THE VICTORIAN AGE IN LITERATURE

BY

G. K. CHESTERTON

Table of Contents

INTRODUCTION..........5
CHAPTER I..........6
   THE VICTORIAN COMPROMISE AND ITS ENEMIES
CHAPTER II..........28
   THE GREAT VICTORIAN NOVELISTS
CHAPTER III..........46
   THE GREAT VICTORIAN POETS
CHAPTER IV..........60
   THE BREAK-UP OF THE COMPROMISE
BIBLIOGRAPHICAL NOTE..........74

INTRODUCTION

A section of a long and splendid literature can be most conveniently treated in one of two ways. It can be divided as one cuts a currant cake or a Gruyère cheese, taking the currants (or the holes) as they come. Or it can be divided as one cuts wood—along the grain: if one thinks that there is a grain. But the two are never the same: the names never come in the same order in actual time as they come in any serious study of a spirit or a tendency. The critic who wishes to move onward with the life of an epoch, must be always running backwards and forwards among its mere dates; just as a branch bends back and forth continually; yet the grain in the branch runs true like an unbroken river.

Mere chronological order, indeed, is almost as arbitrary as alphabetical order. To deal with Darwin, Dickens, Browning, in the sequence of the birthday book would be to forge about as real a chain as the "Tacitus, Tolstoy, Tupper" of a biographical dictionary. It might lend itself more, perhaps, to accuracy: and it might satisfy that school of critics who hold that every artist should be treated as a solitary craftsman, indifferent to the commonwealth and unconcerned about moral things. To write on that principle in the present case, however, would involve all those delicate difficulties, known to politicians, which beset the public defence of a doctrine which one heartily disbelieves. It is quite needless here to go into the old "art for art's sake"—business, or explain at length why individual artists cannot be reviewed without reference to their traditions and creeds. It is enough to say that with other creeds they would have been, for literary purposes, other individuals. Their views do not, of course, make the brains in their heads any more than the ink in their pens. But it is equally evident that mere brain-power, without attributes or aims, a wheel revolving in the void, would be a subject about as entertaining as ink. The moment we differentiate the minds, we must differentiate by doctrines and moral sentiments. A mere sympathy for democratic merry-making and mourning will not make a man a writer like Dickens. But without that sympathy Dickens would not be a writer like Dickens; and probably not a writer at all. A mere conviction that Catholic thought is the clearest as well as the best disciplined, will not make a man a writer like Newman. But without that conviction Newman would not be a writer like Newman; and probably not a writer at all. It is useless for the æsthete (or any other anarchist) to urge the isolated individuality of the artist, apart from his attitude to his age. His attitude to his age is his individuality: men are never individual when alone.

It only remains for me, therefore, to take the more delicate and entangled task; and deal with the great Victorians, not only by dates and names, but rather by schools and streams of thought. It is a task for which I feel myself wholly incompetent; but as that applies to every other literary enterprise I ever went in for, the sensation is not wholly novel: indeed, it is rather reassuring than otherwise to realise that I am now doing something that nobody could do properly. The chief peril of the process, however, will be an inevitable tendency to make the spiritual landscape too large for the figures. I must ask for indulgence if such criticism traces too far back into politics or ethics the roots of which great books were the blossoms; makes Utilitarianism more important than *Liberty* or talks more of the Oxford Movement than of *The Christian Year*. I can only answer in the very temper of the age of which I write: for I also was born a Victorian; and sympathise not a little with the serious Victorian spirit. I can only answer, I shall not make religion more important than it was to Keble, or politics more sacred than they were to Mill.

CHAPTER I

THE VICTORIAN COMPROMISE AND ITS ENEMIES

The previous literary life of this country had left vigorous many old forces in the Victorian time, as in our time. Roman Britain and Mediæval England are still not only alive but lively; for real development is not leaving things behind, as on a road, but drawing life from them, as from a root. Even when we improve we never progress. For progress, the metaphor from the road, implies a man leaving his home behind him: but improvement means a man exalting the towers or extending the gardens of his home. The ancient English literature was like all the several literatures of Christendom, alike in its likeness, alike in its very unlikeness. Like all European cultures, it was European; like all European cultures, it was something more than European. A most marked and unmanageable national temperament is plain in Chaucer and the ballads of Robin Hood; in spite of deep and sometimes disastrous changes of national policy, that note is still unmistakable in Shakespeare, in Johnson and his friends, in Cobbett, in Dickens. It is vain to dream of defining such vivid things; a national soul is as indefinable as a smell, and as unmistakable. I remember a friend who tried impatiently to explain the word "mistletoe" to a German, and cried at last, despairing, "Well, you know holly—mistletoe's the opposite!" I do not commend this logical method in the comparison of plants or nations. But if he had said to the Teuton, "Well, you know Germany—England's the opposite"—the definition, though fallacious, would not have been wholly false. England, like all Christian countries, absorbed valuable elements from the forests and the rude romanticism of the North; but, like all Christian countries, it drank its longest literary draughts from the classic fountains of the ancients: nor was this (as is so often loosely thought) a matter of the mere "Renaissance." The English tongue and talent of speech did not merely flower suddenly into the gargantuan polysyllables of the great Elizabethans; it had always been full of the popular Latin of the Middle Ages. But whatever balance of blood and racial idiom one allows, it is really true that the only suggestion that gets near the Englishman is to hint how far he is from the German. The Germans, like the Welsh, can sing perfectly serious songs perfectly seriously in chorus: can with clear eyes and clear voices join together in words of innocent and beautiful personal passion, for a false maiden or a dead child. The nearest one can get to defining the poetic temper of Englishmen is to say that they couldn't do this even for beer. They can sing in chorus, and louder than other Christians: but they must have in their songs something, I know not what, that is at once shamefaced and rowdy. If the matter be emotional, it must somehow be also broad, common and comic, as "Wapping Old Stairs" and "Sally in Our Alley." If it be patriotic, it must somehow be openly bombastic and, as it were, indefensible, like "Rule Britannia" or like that superb song (I never knew its name, if it has one) that records the number of leagues from Ushant to the Scilly Isles. Also there is a tender love-lyric called "O Tarry Trousers" which is even more English than the heart of *The Midsummer Night's Dream*. But our greatest bards and sages have often shown a tendency to rant it and roar it like true British sailors; to employ an extravagance that is half conscious and therefore half humorous. Compare, for example, the rants of Shakespeare with the rants of Victor Hugo. A piece of Hugo's eloquence is either a serious triumph or a serious collapse: one feels the poet is offended at a smile. But Shakespeare seems rather proud of talking nonsense: I never can read that rousing and mounting description of the storm, where it comes to—

"Who take the ruffian billows by the top,
Curling their monstrous heads, and *hanging* them
With deafening clamour in the slippery clouds."

without seeing an immense balloon rising from the ground, with Shakespeare grinning over the edge of the car, and saying, "You can't stop me: I am above reason now." That is the nearest we can get to the general national spirit, which we have now to follow through one brief and curious but very national episode.

Three years before the young queen was crowned, William Cobbett was buried at Farnham. It may seem strange to begin with this great neglected name, rather than the old age of Wordsworth or the young death of Shelley. But to any one who feels literature as human, the empty chair of Cobbett is more solemn and significant than the throne. With him died the sort of democracy that was a return to Nature, and which only poets and mobs can understand. After him Radicalism is urban—and Toryism suburban. Going through green Warwickshire, Cobbett might have thought of the crops and Shelley of the clouds. But Shelley would have called Birmingham what Cobbett called it—a hell-hole. Cobbett was one with after Liberals in the ideal of Man under an equal law, a citizen of no mean city. He differed from after Liberals in strongly affirming that Liverpool and Leeds are mean cities.

It is no idle Hibernianism to say that towards the end of the eighteenth century the most important event in English history happened in France. It would seem still more perverse, yet it would be still more precise, to say that the most important event in English history was the event that never happened at all—the English Revolution on the lines of the French Revolution. Its failure was not due to any lack of fervour or even ferocity in those who would have brought it about:

from the time when the first shout went up for Wilkes to the time when the last Luddite fires were quenched in a cold rain of rationalism, the spirit of Cobbett, of rural republicanism, of English and patriotic democracy, burned like a beacon. The revolution failed because it was foiled by another revolution; an aristocratic revolution, a victory of the rich over the poor. It was about this time that the common lands were finally enclosed; that the more cruel game laws were first established; that England became finally a land of landlords instead of common land-owners. I will not call it a Tory reaction; for much of the worst of it (especially of the land-grabbing) was done by Whigs; but we may certainly call it Anti-Jacobin. Now this fact, though political, is not only relevant but essential to everything that concerned literature. The upshot was that though England was full of the revolutionary ideas, nevertheless there was no revolution. And the effect of this in turn was that from the middle of the eighteenth century to the middle of the nineteenth the spirit of revolt in England took a wholly literary form. In France it was what people did that was wild and elemental; in England it was what people wrote. It is a quaint comment on the notion that the English are practical and the French merely visionary, that we were rebels in arts while they were rebels in arms.

It has been well and wittily said (as illustrating the mildness of English and the violence of French developments) that the same Gospel of Rousseau which in France produced the Terror, in England produced *Sandford and Merton*. But people forget that in literature the English were by no means restrained by Mr. Barlow; and that if we turn from politics to art, we shall find the two parts peculiarly reversed. It would be equally true to say that the same eighteenth-century emancipation which in France produced the pictures of David, in England produced the pictures of Blake. There never were, I think, men who gave to the imagination so much of the sense of having broken out into the very borderlands of being, as did the great English poets of the romantic or revolutionary period; than Coleridge in the secret sunlight of the Antarctic, where the waters were like witches' oils; than Keats looking out of those extreme mysterious casements upon that ultimate sea. The heroes and criminals of the great French crisis would have been quite as incapable of such imaginative independence as Keats and Coleridge would have been incapable of winning the battle of Wattignies. In Paris the tree of liberty was a garden tree, clipped very correctly; and Robespierre used the razor more regularly than the guillotine. Danton, who knew and admired English literature, would have cursed freely over *Kubla Khan*; and if the Committee of Public Safety had not already executed Shelley as an aristocrat, they would certainly have locked him up for a madman. Even Hébert (the one really vile Revolutionist), had he been reproached by English poets with worshipping the Goddess of Reason, might legitimately have retorted that it was rather the Goddess of Unreason that they set up to be worshipped. Verbally considered, Carlyle's *French Revolution* was more revolutionary than the real French Revolution: and if Carrier, in an exaggerative phrase, empurpled the Loire with carnage, Turner almost literally set the Thames on fire.

This trend of the English Romantics to carry out the revolutionary idea not savagely in works, but very wildly indeed in words, had several results; the most important of which was this. It started English literature after the Revolution with a sort of bent towards independence and eccentricity, which in the brighter wits became individuality, and in the duller ones, Individualism. English Romantics, English Liberals, were not public men making a republic, but poets, each seeing a vision. The lonelier version of liberty was a sort of aristocratic anarchism in Byron and Shelley; but though in Victorian times it faded into much milder prejudices and much more *bourgeois* crotchets, England retained from that twist a certain odd separation and privacy. England became much more of an island than she had ever been before. There fell from her about this time, not only the understanding of France or Germany, but to her own long and yet lingering disaster, the understanding of Ireland. She had not joined in the attempt to create European democracy; nor did she, save in the first glow of Waterloo, join in the counter-attempt to destroy it. The life in her literature was still, to a large extent, the romantic liberalism of Rousseau, the free and humane truisms that had refreshed the other nations, the return to Nature and to natural rights. But that which in Rousseau was a creed, became in Hazlitt a taste and in Lamb little more than a whim. These latter and their like form a group at the beginning of the nineteenth century of those we may call the Eccentrics: they gather round Coleridge and his decaying dreams or linger in the tracks of Keats and Shelley and Godwin; Lamb with his bibliomania and creed of pure caprice, the most unique of all geniuses; Leigh Hunt with his Bohemian impecuniosity; Landor with his tempestuous temper, throwing plates on the floor; Hazlitt with his bitterness and his low love affair; even that healthier and happier Bohemian, Peacock. With these, in one sense at least, goes De Quincey. He was, unlike most of these embers of the revolutionary age in letters, a Tory; and was attached to the political army which is best represented in letters by the virile laughter and leisure of Wilson's *Noctes Ambrosianæ*. But he had nothing in common with that environment. It remained for some time as a Tory tradition, which balanced the cold and brilliant aristocracy of the Whigs. It lived on the legend of Trafalgar; the sense that insularity was independence; the sense that anomalies are as jolly as family jokes; the general sense that old salts are the salt of the earth. It still lives in some old songs about Nelson or Waterloo, which are vastly more pompous and vastly more sincere than the cockney cocksureness of later Jingo lyrics. But it is hard to connect De Quincey with it; or, indeed, with anything else. De Quincey would certainly have been a happier man, and almost certainly a better man, if he had got drunk on toddy with Wilson, instead of getting calm and clear (as he himself describes) on opium, and with no company but a book of German metaphysics. But he would hardly have revealed those wonderful vistas and perspectives of prose, which permit one to call him the first and most powerful of the decadents: those sentences that lengthen out like nightmare corridors, or rise higher and higher like impossible eastern pagodas. He was a morbid fellow, and far less moral than Burns; for when Burns confessed excess he did not defend it. But he has cast a gigantic shadow on our literature, and was as certainly a genius as Poe. Also he had humour, which Poe had not. And if any one still smarting from the pinpricks of Wilde or Whistler, wants to convict them of plagiarism in their "art for art" epigrams—he will find most of what they said said better in *Murder as One of the Fine Arts*.

One great man remains of this elder group, who did their last work only under Victoria; he knew most of the members of it, yet he did not belong to it in any corporate sense. He was a poor man and an invalid, with Scotch blood and a strong, though perhaps only inherited, quarrel with the old Calvinism; by name Thomas Hood. Poverty and illness forced him to the toils of an incessant jester; and the revolt against gloomy religion made him turn his wit, whenever he could, in the direction of a defence of happier and humaner views. In the long great roll that includes Homer and Shakespeare, he was the last great man who really employed the pun. His puns were not all good (nor were Shakespeare's), but the best of them were a strong and fresh form of art. The pun is said to be a thing of two meanings; but with Hood there were three meanings, for there was also the abstract truth that would have been there with no pun at all. The pun of Hood is underrated, like the "wit" of Voltaire, by those who forget that the words of Voltaire were not pins, but swords. In Hood at his best the verbal neatness only gives to the satire or the scorn a ring of finality such as is given by rhyme. For rhyme does go with reason, since the aim of both is to bring things to an end. The tragic necessity of puns tautened and hardened Hood's genius; so that there is always a sort of shadow of that sharpness across all his serious poems, falling like the shadow of a sword. "Sewing at once with a double thread a shroud as well as a shirt"—"We thought her dying when she slept, and sleeping when she died"—"Oh God, that bread should be so dear and flesh and blood so cheap"— none can fail to note in these a certain fighting discipline of phrase, a compactness and point which was well trained in lines like "A cannon-ball took off his legs, so he laid down his arms." In France he would have been a great epigrammatist, like Hugo. In England he is a punster.

There was nothing at least in this group I have loosely called the Eccentrics that disturbs the general sense that all their generation was part of the sunset of the great revolutionary poets. This fading glamour affected England in a sentimental and, to some extent, a snobbish direction; making men feel that great lords with long curls and whiskers were naturally the wits that led the world. But it affected England also negatively and by reaction; for it associated such men as Byron with superiority, but not with success. The English middle classes were led to distrust poetry almost as much as they admired it. They could not believe that either vision at the one end or violence at the other could ever be practical. They were deaf to that great warning of Hugo: "You say the poet is in the clouds; but so is the thunderbolt." Ideals exhausted themselves in the void; Victorian England, very unwisely, would have no more to do with idealists in politics. And this, chiefly, because there had been about these great poets a young and splendid sterility; since the pantheist Shelley was in fact washed under by the wave of the world, or Byron sank in death as he drew the sword for Hellas.

The chief turn of nineteenth-century England was taken about the time when a footman at Holland House opened a door and announced "Mr. Macaulay."

Macaulay's literary popularity was representative and it was deserved; but his presence among the great Whig families marks an epoch. He was the son of one of the first "friends of the negro," whose honest industry and philanthropy were darkened by a religion of sombre smugness, which almost makes one fancy they loved the negro for his colour, and would have turned away from red or yellow men as needlessly gaudy. But his wit and his politics (combined with that dropping of the Puritan tenets but retention of the Puritan tone which marked his class and generation), lifted him into a sphere which was utterly opposite to that from which he came. This Whig world was exclusive; but it was not narrow. It was very difficult for an outsider to get into it; but if he did get into it he was in a much freer atmosphere than any other in England. Of those aristocrats, the Old Guard of the eighteenth century, many denied God, many defended Bonaparte, and nearly all sneered at the Royal Family. Nor did wealth or birth make any barriers for those once within this singular Whig world. The platform was high, but it was level. Moreover the upstart nowadays pushes himself by wealth: but the Whigs could choose their upstarts. In that world Macaulay found Rogers, with his phosphorescent and corpse-like brilliancy; there he found Sydney Smith, bursting with crackers of common sense, an admirable old heathen; there he found Tom Moore, the romantic of the Regency, a shortened shadow of Lord Byron. That he reached this platform and remained on it is, I say, typical of a turning-point in the century. For the fundamental fact of early Victorian history was this: the decision of the middle classes to employ their new wealth in backing up a sort of aristocratical compromise, and not (like the middle class in the French Revolution) insisting on a clean sweep and a clear democratic programme. It went along with the decision of the aristocracy to recruit itself more freely from the middle class. It was then also that Victorian "prudery" began: the great lords yielded on this as on Free Trade. These two decisions have made the doubtful England of to-day; and Macaulay is typical of them; he is the *bourgeois* in Belgravia. The alliance is marked by his great speeches for Lord Grey's Reform Bill: it is marked even more significantly in his speech against the Chartists. Cobbett was dead.

Macaulay makes the foundation of the Victorian age in all its very English and unique elements: its praise of Puritan politics and abandonment of Puritan theology; its belief in a cautious but perpetual patching up of the Constitution; its admiration for industrial wealth. But above all he typifies the two things that really make the Victorian Age itself, the cheapness and narrowness of its conscious formulæ; the richness and humanity of its unconscious tradition. There were two Macaulays, a rational Macaulay who was generally wrong, and a romantic Macaulay who was almost invariably right. All that was small in him derives from the dull parliamentarism of men like Sir James Mackintosh; but all that was great in him has much more kinship with the festive antiquarianism of Sir Walter Scott.

As a philosopher he had only two thoughts; and neither of them is true. The first was that politics, as an experimental science, must go on improving, along with clocks, pistols or penknives, by the mere accumulation of experiment and variety.

He was, indeed, far too strong-minded a man to accept the hazy modern notion that the soul in its highest sense can change: he seems to have held that religion can never get any better and that poetry rather tends to get worse. But he did not see the flaw in his political theory; which is that unless the soul improves with time there is no guarantee that the accumulations of experience will be adequately used. Figures do not add themselves up; birds do not label or stuff themselves; comets do not calculate their own courses; these things are done by the soul of man. And if the soul of man is subject to other laws, is liable to sin, to sleep, to anarchism or to suicide, then all sciences including politics may fall as sterile and lie as fallow as before man's reason was made. Macaulay seemed sometimes to talk as if clocks produced clocks, or guns had families of little pistols, or a penknife littered like a pig. The other view he held was the more or less utilitarian theory of toleration; that we should get the best butcher whether he was a Baptist or a Muggletonian, and the best soldier whether he was a Wesleyan or an Irvingite. The compromise worked well enough in an England Protestant in bulk; but Macaulay ought to have seen that it has its limitations. A good butcher might be a Baptist; he is not very likely to be a Buddhist. A good soldier might be a Wesleyan; he would hardly be a Quaker. For the rest, Macaulay was concerned to interpret the seventeenth century in terms of the triumph of the Whigs as champions of public rights; and he upheld this one-sidedly but not malig nantly in a style of rounded and ringing sentences, which at its best is like steel and at its worst like tin.

This was the small conscious Macaulay; the great unconscious Macaulay was very different. His noble enduring quality in our literature is this: that he truly had an abstract passion for history; a warm, poetic and sincere enthusiasm for great things as such; an ardour and appetite for great books, great battles, great cities, great men. He felt and used names like trumpets. The reader's greatest joy is in the writer's own joy, when he can let his last phrase fall like a hammer on some resounding name like Hildebrand or Charlemagne, on the eagles of Rome or the pillars of Hercules. As with Walter Scott, some of the best things in his prose and poetry are the surnames that he did not make. And it is remarkable to notice that this romance of history, so far from making him more partial or untrustworthy, was the only thing that made him moderately just. His reason was entirely one-sided and fanatical. It was his imagination that was well-balanced and broad. He was monotonously certain that only Whigs were right; but it was necessary that Tories should at least be great, that his heroes might have foemen worthy of their steel. If there was one thing in the world he hated it was a High Church Royalist parson; yet when Jeremy Collier the Jacobite priest raises a real banner, all Macaulay's blood warms with the mere prospect of a fight. "It is inspiriting to see how gallantly the solitary outlaw advances to attack enemies formidable separately, and, it might have been thought, irresistible when combined; distributes his swashing blows right and left among Wycherley, Congreve and Vanbrugh, treads the wretched D'Urfey down in the dirt beneath his feet; and strikes with all his strength full at the towering crest of Dryden." That is exactly where Macaulay is great; because he is almost Homeric. The whole triumph turns upon mere names; but men are commanded by names. So his poem on the Armada is really a good geography book gone mad; one sees the map of England come alive and march and mix under the eye.

The chief tragedy in the trend of later literature may be expressed by saying that the smaller Macaulay conquered the larger. Later men had less and less of that hot love of history he had inherited from Scott. They had more and more of that cold science of self-interests which he had learnt from Bentham.

The name of this great man, though it belongs to a period before the Victorian, is, like the name of Cobbett, very important to it. In substance Macaulay accepted the conclusions of Bentham; though he offered brilliant objections to all his arguments. In any case the soul of Bentham (if he had one) went marching on, like John Brown; and in the central Victorian movement it was certainly he who won. John Stuart Mill was the final flower of that growth. He was himself fresh and delicate and pure; but that is the business of a flower. Though he had to preach a hard rationalism in religion, a hard competition in economics, a hard egoism in ethics, his own soul had all that silvery sensitiveness that can be seen in his fine portrait by Watts. He boasted none of that brutal optimism with which his friends and followers of the Manchester School expounded their cheery negations. There was about Mill even a sort of embarrassment; he exhibited all the wheels of his iron universe rather reluctantly, like a gentleman in trade showing ladies over his factory. There shone in him a beautiful reverence for women, which is all the more touching because, in his department, as it were, he could only offer them so dry a gift as the Victorian Parliamentary Franchise.

Now in trying to describe how the Victorian writers stood to each other, we must recur to the very real difficulty noted at the beginning: the difficulty of keeping the moral order parallel with the chronological order. For the mind moves by instincts, associations, premonitions and not by fixed dates or completed processes. Action and reaction will occur simultaneously: or the cause actually be found after the effect. Errors will be resisted before they have been properly promulgated: notions will be first defined long after they are dead. It is no good getting the almanac to look up moonshine; and most literature in this sense is moonshine. Thus Wordsworth shrank back into Toryism, as it were, from a Shelleyan extreme of pantheism as yet disembodied. Thus Newman took down the iron sword of dogma to parry a blow not yet delivered, that was coming from the club of Darwin. For this reason no one can understand tradition, or even history, who has not some tenderness for anachronism.

Now for the great part of the Victorian era the utilitarian tradition which reached its highest in Mill held the centre of the field; it was the philosophy in office, so to speak. It sustained its march of codification and inquiry until it had made possible the great victories of Darwin and Huxley and Wallace. If we take Macaulay at the beginning of the epoch and Huxley at the end of it, we shall find that they had much in common. They were both square-jawed, simple men, greedy of controversy but scornful of sophistry, dead to mysticism but very much alive to morality; and they were both very much more under the influence of their own admirable rhetoric than they knew. Huxley, especially, was much more a literary than a scientific man. It is amusing to note that when Huxley was charged with being rhetorical, he expressed his horror of "plastering the fair face of truth with that pestilent cosmetic, rhetoric," which is itself about as well-plastered a piece of rhetoric as Ruskin himself could have managed. The difference that the period had developed can best be seen if we consider this: that while neither was of a spiritual sort, Macaulay took it for granted that common sense required some kind of theology, while Huxley took it for granted that common sense meant having none. Macaulay, it is said, never talked about his religion: but Huxley was always talking about the religion he hadn't got.

But though this simple Victorian rationalism held the centre, and in a certain sense *was* the Victorian era, it was assailed on many sides, and had been assailed even before the beginning of that era. The rest of the intellectual history of the time is a series of reactions against it, which come wave after wave. They have succeeded in shaking it, but not in dislodging it from the modern mind. The first of these was the Oxford Movement; a bow that broke when it had let loose the flashing arrow that was Newman. The second reaction was one man; without teachers or pupils—Dickens. The third reaction was a group that tried to create a sort of new romantic Protestantism, to pit against both Reason and Rome—Carlyle, Ruskin, Kingsley, Maurice—perhaps Tennyson. Browning also was at once romantic and Puritan; but he belonged to no group, and worked against materialism in a manner entirely his own. Though as a boy he bought eagerly Shelley's revolutionary poems, he did not think of becoming a revolutionary poet. He concentrated on the special souls of men; seeking God in a series of private interviews. Hence Browning, great as he is, is rather one of the Victorian novelists than wholly of the Victorian poets. From Ruskin, again, descend those who may be called the Pre-Raphaelites of prose and poetry.

It is really with this rationalism triumphant, and with the romance of these various attacks on it, that the study of Victorian literature begins and proceeds. Bentham was already the prophet of a powerful sect; Macaulay was already the historian of an historic party, before the true Victorian epoch began. The middle classes were emerging in a state of damaged Puritanism. The upper classes were utterly pagan. Their clear and courageous testimony remains in those immortal words of Lord Melbourne, who had led the young queen to the throne and long stood there as her protector. "No one has more respect for the Christian religion than I have; but really, when it comes to intruding it into private life——" What was pure paganism in the politics of Melbourne became a sort of mystical cynicism in the politics of Disraeli; and is well mirrored in his novels—for he was a man who felt at home in mirrors. With every allowance for aliens and eccentrics and all the accidents that must always eat the edges of any systematic circumference, it may still be said that the Utilitarians held the fort.

Of the Oxford Movement what remains most strongly in the Victorian Epoch centres round the challenge of Newman, its one great literary man. But the movement as a whole had been of great significance in the very genesis and make up of the society: yet that significance is not quite easy immediately to define. It was certainly not æsthetic ritualism; scarcely one of the Oxford High

Churchmen was what we should call a Ritualist. It was certainly not a conscious reaching out towards Rome: except on a Roman Catholic theory which might explain all our unrests by that dim desire. It knew little of Europe, it knew nothing of Ireland, to which any merely Roman Catholic revulsion would obviously have turned. In the first instance, I think, the more it is studied, the more it would appear that it was a movement of mere religion as such. It was not so much a taste for Catholic dogma, but simply a hunger for dogma. For dogma means the serious satisfaction of the mind. Dogma does not mean the absence of thought, but the end of thought. It was a revolt against the Victorian spirit in one particular aspect of it; which may roughly be called (in a cosy and domestic Victorian metaphor) having your cake and eating it too. It saw that the solid and serious Victorians were fundamentally frivo lous—because they were fundamentally inconsistent.

A man making the confession of any creed worth ten minutes' intelligent talk, is always a man who gains something and gives up something. So long as he does both he can create: for he is making an outline and a shape. Mahomet created, when he forbade wine but allowed five wives: he created a very big thing, which we have still to deal with. The first French Republic created, when it affirmed property and abolished peerages; France still stands like a square, four-sided building which Europe has besieged in vain. The men of the Oxford Movement would have been horrified at being compared either with Moslems or Jacobins. But their sub-conscious thirst was for something that Moslems and Jacobins had and ordinary Anglicans had not: the exalted excitement of consistency. If you were a Moslem you were not a Bacchanal. If you were a Republican you were not a peer. And so the Oxford men, even in their first and dimmest stages, felt that if you were a Churchman you were not a Dissenter. The Oxford Movement was, out of the very roots of its being, a rational movement; almost a rationalist movement. In that it differed sharply from the other reactions that shook the Utilitarian compromise; the blinding mysticism of Carlyle, the mere manly emotionalism of Dickens. It was an appeal to reason: reason said that if a Christian had a feast day he must have a fast day too. Otherwise, all days ought to be alike; and this was that very Utilitarianism against which their Oxford Movement was the first and most rational assault.

This idea, even by reason of its reason, narrowed into a sort of sharp spear, of which the spear blade was Newman. It did forget many of the other forces that were fighting on its side. But the movement could boast, first and last, many men who had this eager dogmatic quality: Keble, who spoilt a poem in order to recognise a doctrine; Faber, who told the rich, almost with taunts, that God sent the poor as eagles to strip them; Froude, who with Newman announced his return in the arrogant motto of Achilles. But the greater part of all this happened before what is properly our period; and in that period Newman, and perhaps Newman alone, is the expression and summary of the whole school. It was certainly in the Victorian Age, and after his passage to Rome, that Newman claimed his complete right to be in any book on modern English literature. This is no place for estimating his theology: but one point about it does clearly emerge. Whatever else is right, the theory that Newman went over to Rome to find peace and an end of argument, is quite unquestionably wrong. He had far more quarrels after he had gone over to Rome. But, though he had far more quarrels, he had far fewer compromises: and he was of that temper which is tortured more by compromise than by quarrel. He was a man at once of abnormal energy and abnormal sensibility: nobody without that combination could have written the *Apologia*. If he sometimes seemed to skin his enemies alive, it was because he himself lacked a skin. In this sense his *Apologia* is a triumph far beyond the ephemeral charge on which it was founded; in this sense he does indeed (to use his own expression) vanquish not his accuser but his judges. Many men would shrink from recording all their cold fits and hesitations and prolonged inconsistencies: I am sure it was the breath of life to Newman to confess them, now that he had done with them for ever. His *Lectures on the Present Position of English Catholics*, practically preached against a raging mob, rise not only higher but happier, as his instant unpopularity increases. There is something grander than humour, there is fun, in the very first lecture about the British Constitution as explained to a meeting of Russians. But always his triumphs are the triumphs of a highly sensitive man: a man must feel insults before he can so insultingly and splendidly avenge them. He is a naked man, who carries a naked sword. The quality of his literary style is so successful that it succeeds in escaping definition. The quality of his logic is that of a long but passionate patience, which waits until he has fixed all corners of an iron trap. But the quality of his moral comment on the age remains what I have said: a protest of the rationality of religion as against the increasing irrationality of mere Victorian comfort and compromise. So far as the present purpose is concerned, his protest died with him: he left few imitators and (it may easily be conceived) no successful imitators. The suggestion of him lingers on in the exquisite Elizabethan perversity of Coventry Patmore; and has later flamed out from the shy volcano of Francis Thompson. Otherwise (as we shall see in the parallel case of Ruskin's Socialism) he has no followers in his own age: but very many in ours.

The next group of reactionaries or romantics or whatever we elect to call them, gathers roughly around one great name. Scotland, from which had come so many of those harsh economists who made the first Radical philosophies of the Victorian Age, was destined also to fling forth (I had almost said to spit forth) their fiercest and most extraordinary enemy. The two primary things in Thomas Carlyle were his early Scotch education and his later German culture. The first was in almost all respects his strength; the latter in some respects his weakness. As an ordinary lowland peasant, he inherited the really valuable historic property of the Scots, their independence, their fighting spirit, and their instinctive philosophic consideration of men merely as men. But he was not an ordinary peasant. If he had laboured obscurely in his village till death, he would have been yet locally a marked man; a man with a wild eye, a man with an air of silent anger; perhaps a man at whom stones were sometimes thrown. A strain of disease and suffering ran athwart both his body and his soul. In spite of his praise of silence, it was only through his gift of utterance that he escaped madness. But while his fellow-peasants would have seen this in him and perhaps mocked it, they would also have seen something which they always expect in such men, and they would have got it: vision, a power in the mind akin to second sight. Like many ungainly or otherwise unattractive Scotchmen, he was a seer. By which I do not mean to refer so much to his transcendental rhapsodies about the World-soul or the Nature-garment or the Mysteries and Eternities generally, these seem to me to belong more to his German side and to be less sincere and vital. I mean a real power of seeing things suddenly, not apparently reached by any process; a grand power of guessing. He *saw* the crowd of the new States General, Danton with his "rude flattened face," Robespierre peering mistily through his spectacles. He *saw* the English charge at Dunbar. He *guessed* that Mirabeau, however dissipated and diseased, had something sturdy inside him. He *guessed* that Lafayette, however brave and victorious, had nothing inside him. He supported the lawlessness of Cromwell, because across two centuries he almost physically *felt* the feebleness and hopelessness of the moderate Parliamentarians. He said a word of sympathy for the universally vituperated Jacobins of the Mountain, because through thick veils of national prejudice and misrepresentation, he felt the impossibility of the Gironde. He was wrong in denying to Scott the power of being inside his characters: but he really had a good deal of that power himself. It was one of his innumerable and rather provincial crotchets to encourage prose as against poetry. But, as a matter of fact, he himself was much greater considered as a kind of poet than considered as anything else; and the central idea of poetry is the idea of guessing right, like a child.

He first emerged, as it were, as a student and disciple of Goethe. The connection was not wholly fortunate. With much of what Goethe really stood for he was not really in sympathy; but in his own obstinate way, he tried to knock his idol into shape instead of choosing another. He pushed further and further the extravagances of a vivid but very unbalanced and barbaric style, in the praise of a poet who really represented the calmest classicism and the attempt to restore a Hellenic equilibrium in the mind. It is like watching a shaggy Scandinavian decorating a Greek statue washed up by chance on his shores. And while the strength of Goethe was a strength of completion and serenity, which Carlyle not only never found but never even sought, the weaknesses of Goethe were of a sort that did not draw the best out of Carlyle. The one civilised element that the German classicists forgot to put into their beautiful balance was a sense of humour. And great poet as Goethe was, there is to the last something faintly fatuous about his half sceptical, half sentimental self-importance; a Lord Chamberlain of teacup politics; an earnest and elderly flirt; a German of the Germans. Now Carlyle had humour; he had it in his very style, but it never got into his philosophy. His philosophy largely remained a heavy Teutonic idealism, absurdly unaware of the complexity of things; as when he perpetually repeated (as with a kind of flat-footed stamping) that people ought to tell the truth; apparently supposing, to quote Stevenson's phrase, that telling the truth is as easy as blind hookey. Yet, though his general honesty is unquestionable, he was by no means one of those who will give up a fancy under the shock of a fact. If by sheer genius he frequently guessed right, he was not the kind of man to admit easily that he had guessed wrong. His version of Cromwell's filthy cruelties in Ireland, or his impatient slurring over of the most sinister riddle in the morality of Frederick the Great—these passages are, one must frankly say, dis ingenuous. But it is, so to speak, a generous disingenuousness; the heat and momentum of sincere admirations, not the shuffling fear and flattery of the constitutional or patriotic historian. It bears most resemblance to the incurable prejudices of a woman.

For the rest there hovered behind all this transcendental haze a certain presence of old northern paganism; he really had some sympathy with the vast vague gods of that moody but not unmanly Nature-worship which seems to have filled the darkness of the North before the coming of the Roman Eagle or the Christian Cross. This he combined, allowing for certain sceptical omissions, with the grisly Old Testament God he had heard about in the black Sabbaths of his childhood; and so promulgated (against both Rationalists and Catholics) a sort of heathen Puritanism: Protestantism purged of its evidences of Christianity.

His great and real work was the attack on Utilitarianism: which did real good, though there was much that was muddled and dangerous in the historical philosophy which he preached as an alternative. It is his real glory that he was the first to see clearly and say plainly the great truth of our time; that the wealth of the state is not the prosperity of the people. Macaulay and the Mills and all the regular run of the Early Victorians, took it for granted that if Manchester was getting richer, we had got hold of the key to comfort and progress. Carlyle pointed out (with stronger sagacity and humour than he showed on any other question) that it was just as true to say that Manchester was getting poorer as that it was getting richer: or, in other words, that Manchester was not getting richer at all, but only some of the less pleasing people in Manchester. In this matter he is to be noted in connection with national developments much later; for he thus became the first prophet of the Socialists. *Sartor Resartus* is an admirable fantasia; *The French Revolution* is, with all its faults, a really fine piece of history; the lectures on Heroes contain some masterly sketches of personalities. But I think it is in *Past and Present*, and the essay on *Chartism*, that Carlyle achieves the work he was chosen by gods and men to achieve; which possibly might not have been achieved by a happier or more healthy-minded man. He never rose to more deadly irony than in such *macabre* descriptions as that of the poor woman proving her sisterhood with the rich by giving them all typhoid fever; or that perfect piece of *badinage* about "Overproduction of Shirts"; in which he imagines the aristocrats claiming to be quite clear of this offence. "Will you bandy accusations, will you accuse *us* of overproduction? We take the Heavens and the Earth to witness that we have produced nothing at all.... He that accuses us of producing, let him show himself. Let him say what and when." And he never wrote so sternly and justly as when he compared the "divine sorrow" of Dante with the "undivine sorrow" of Utilitarianism, which had already come down to talking about the breeding of the poor and to hinting at infanticide. This is a representative quarrel; for if the Utilitarian spirit reached its highest point in Mill, it certainly reached its lowest point in Malthus.

One last element in the influence of Carlyle ought to be mentioned; because it very strongly dominated his disciples—especially Kingsley, and to some extent Tennyson and Ruskin. Because he frowned at the cockney cheerfulness of the cheaper economists, they and others represented him as a pessimist, and reduced all his azure infinities to a fit of the blues. But Carlyle's philosophy, more carefully considered, will be found to be dangerously optimist rather than pessimist. As a thinker Carlyle is not sad, but recklessly and rather unscrupulously satisfied. For he seems to have held the theory that good could not be definitely defeated in this world; and that everything in the long run finds its right level. It began with what we may call the "Bible of History" idea: that all affairs and politics were a clouded but unbroken revelation of the divine. Thus any enormous and unaltered human settlement—as the Norman Conquest or the secession of America—we must suppose to be the will of God. It lent itself to picturesque treatment; and Carlyle and the Carlyleans were above all things picturesque. It gave them at first a rhetorical advantage over the Catholic and other older schools. They could boast that their Creator was still creating; that he was in Man and Nature, and was not hedged round in a Paradise or imprisoned in a pyx. They could say their God had not grown too old for war: that He was present at Gettysburg and Gravelotte as much as at Gibeon and Gilboa. I do not mean that they literally said these particular things: they are what I should have said had I been bribed to defend their position. But they said things to the same effect: that what manages finally to happen, happens for a higher purpose. Car lyle said the French Revolution was a thing settled in the eternal councils to be; and therefore (and not because it was right) attacking it was "fighting against God." And Kingsley even carried the principle so far as to tell a lady she should remain in the Church of England mainly because God had put her there. But in spite of its superficial spirituality and encouragement, it is not hard to see how such a doctrine could be abused. It practically comes to saying that God is on the side of the big battalions—or at least, of the victorious ones. Thus a creed which set out to create conquerors would only corrupt soldiers; corrupt them with a craven and unsoldierly worship of success: and that which began as the philosophy of courage ends as the philosophy of cowardice. If, indeed, Carlyle were right in saying that right is only "rightly articulated" might, men would never articulate or move in any way. For no act can have might before it is done: if there is no right, it cannot rationally be done at all. This element, like the Anti-Utilitarian element, is to be kept in mind in connection with after developments: for in this Carlyle is the first cry of Imperialism, as (in the other case) of Socialism: and the two babes unborn who stir at the trumpet are Mr. Bernard Shaw and Mr. Rudyard Kipling. Kipling also carries on from Carlyle the concentration on the purely Hebraic parts of the Bible. The fallacy of this whole philosophy is that if God is indeed present at a modern battle, He may be present not as on Gilboa but Golgotha.

Carlyle's direct historical worship of strength and the rest of it was fortunately not very fruitful; and perhaps lingered only in Froude the historian. Even he is more an interruption than a continuity. Froude develops rather the harsher and more impatient moral counsels of his master than like Ruskin the more romantic and sympathetic. He carries on the tradition of Hero Worship: but carries far beyond Carlyle the practice of worshipping people who cannot rationally be called heroes. In this matter that eccentric eye of the seer certainly helped Carlyle: in Cromwell and Frederick the Great there was at least something self-begotten, original or mystical; if they were not heroes they were at least demigods or perhaps demons. But Froude set himself to the praise of the Tudors, a much lower class of people; ill-conditioned prosperous people who merely waxed fat and kicked. Such strength as Henry VIII had was the strength of a badly trained horse that bolts, not of any clear or courageous rider who controls him. There is a sort of strong man mentioned in Scripture who, because he masters himself, is more than he that takes a city. There is another kind of strong man (known to the medical profession) who cannot master himself; and whom it may take half a city to take alive. But for all that he is a low lunatic, and not a hero; and of that sort were too many of the heroes whom Froude attempted to praise. A kind of instinct kept Carlyle from over-praising Henry VIII; or that highly cultivated and complicated liar, Queen Elizabeth. Here, the only importance of this is that one of Carlyle's followers carried further that "strength" which was the real weakness of Carlyle. I have heard that Froude's life of Carlyle was unsympathetic; but if it was so it was a sort of parricide. For the rest, like Macaulay, he was a picturesque and partisan historian: but, like Macaulay (and unlike the craven scientific historians of to-day) he was not ashamed of being partisan or of being picturesque. Such studies as he wrote on the Elizabethan seamen and adventurers, represent very triumphantly the sort of romance of England that all this school was attempting to establish; and link him up with Kingsley and the rest.

Ruskin may be very roughly regarded as the young lieutenant of Carlyle in his war on Utilitarian Radicalism: but as an individual he presents many and curious divergences. In the matter of style, he enriched English without disordering it. And in the matter of religion (which was the key of this age as of every other) he did not, like Carlyle, set up the romance of the great Puritans as a rival to the romance of the Catholic Church. Rather he set up and worshipped all the arts and trophies of the Catholic Church as a rival to the Church itself. None need dispute that he held a perfectly tenable position if he chose to associate early Florentine art with a Christianity still comparatively pure, and such sensualities as the Renaissance bred with the corruption of a Papacy. But this does not alter, as a merely artistic fact, the strange air of ill-ease and irritation with which Ruskin seems to tear down the gargoyles of Amiens or the marbles of Venice, as things of which Europe is not worthy; and take them away with him to a really careful museum, situated dangerously near Clapham. Many of the great men of that generation, indeed, had a sort of divided mind; an ethical headache which was literally a "splitting headache"; for there was a schism in the sympathies. When these men looked at some historic object, like the Catholic Church or the French Revolution, they did not know whether they loved or hated it most. Carlyle's two eyes were out of focus, as one may say, when he looked at democracy: he had one eye on Valmy and the other on Sedan. In the same way, Ruskin had a strong right hand that wrote of the great mediæval minsters in tall harmonies and traceries as splendid as their own; and also, so to speak, a weak and feverish left hand that was always fidgeting and trying to take the pen away —and write an evangelical tract about the immorality of foreigners. Many of their contemporaries were the same. The sea of Tennyson's mind was troubled under its serene surface. The incessant excitement of Kingsley, though romantic and attractive in many ways, was a great deal more like Nervous Christianity than Muscular Christianity. It would be quite unfair to say of Ruskin that there was any major inconsistency between his mediæ val tastes and his very unmediæval temper: and minor inconsistencies do not matter in anybody. But it is not quite unfair to say of him that he seemed to want all parts of the Cathedral except the altar.

As an artist in prose he is one of the most miraculous products of the extremely poetical genius of England. The length of a Ruskin sentence is like that length in the long arrow that was boasted of by the drawers of the long bow. He draws, not a cloth-yard shaft but a long lance to his ear: he shoots a spear. But the whole goes light as a bird and straight as a bullet. There is no Victorian writer before him to whom he even suggests a comparison, technically considered, except perhaps De Quincey; who also employed the long rich rolling sentence that, like a rocket, bursts into stars at the end. But De Quincey's sentences, as I have said, have always a dreamy and insecure sense about them, like the turret on toppling turret of some mad sultan's pagoda. Ruskin's sentence branches into brackets and relative clauses as a straight strong tree branches into boughs and bifurcations, rather shaking off its burden than merely adding to it. It is interesting to remember that Ruskin wrote some of the best of these sentences in the attempt to show that he did understand the growth of trees, and that nobody else did—except Turner, of course. It is also (to those acquainted with his perverse and wild rhetorical prejudices) even more amusing to remember that if a Ruskin sentence (occupying one or two pages of small print) does not remind us of the growth of a tree, the only other thing it does remind of is the triumphant passage of a railway train.

Ruskin left behind him in his turn two quite separate streams of inspiration. The first and more practical was concerned, like Carlyle's *Chartism*, with a challenge to the social conclusions of the orthodox economists. He was not so great a man as Carlyle, but he was a much more clear-headed man; and the point and stab of his challenge still really stands and sticks, like a dagger in a dead man. He answered the theory that we must always get the cheapest labour we can, by pointing out that we never do get the cheapest labour we can, in any matter about which we really care twopence. We do not get the cheapest doctor. We either get a doctor who charges nothing or a doctor who charges a recognised and respectable fee. We do not trust the cheapest bishop. We do not allow admirals to compete. We do not tell generals to undercut each other on the eve of a war. We either employ none of them or we employ all of them at an official rate of pay. All this was set out in the strongest and least sentimental of his books, *Unto this Last*; but many suggestions of it are scattered through *Sesame and Lilies*, *The Political Economy of Art*, and even *Modern Painters*. On this side of his soul Ruskin became the second founder of Socialism. The argument was not by any means a complete or unconquerable weapon, but I think it knocked out what little re mained of the brains of the early Victorian rationalists. It is entirely nonsensical to speak of Ruskin as a lounging æsthete, who strolled into economics, and talked sentimentalism. In plain fact, Ruskin was seldom so sensible and logical (right or wrong) as when he was talking about economics. He constantly talked the most glorious nonsense about landscape and natural history, which it was his business to understand. Within his own limits, he talked the most cold common sense about political economy, which was no business of his at all.

On the other side of his literary soul, his mere unwrapping of the wealth and wonder of European art, he set going another influence, earlier and vaguer than his influence on Socialism. He represented what was at first the Pre-Raphaelite School in painting, but afterwards a much larger and looser Pre-Raphaelite School in poetry and prose. The word "looser" will not be found unfair if we remember how Swinburne and all the wildest friends of the Rossettis carried this movement forward. They used the mediæval imagery to blaspheme the mediæval religion. Ruskin's dark and doubtful decision to accept Catholic art but not Catholic ethics had borne rapid or even flagrant fruit by the time that Swinburne, writing about a harlot, composed a learned and sympathetic and indecent parody on the Litany of the Blessed Virgin.

With the poets I deal in another part of this book; but the influence of Ruskin's great prose touching art criticism can best be expressed in the name of the next great prose writer on such subjects. That name is Walter Pater: and the name is the full measure of the extent to which Ruskin's vague but vast influence had escaped from his hands. Pater eventually joined the Church of Rome (which would not have pleased Ruskin at all), but it is surely fair to say of the mass of his work that its moral tone is neither Puritan nor Catholic, but strictly and splendidly Pagan. In Pater we have Ruskin without the prej udices, that is, without the funny parts. I may be wrong, but I cannot recall at this moment a single passage in which Pater's style takes a holiday or in which his wisdom plays the fool. Newman and Ruskin were as careful and graceful stylists as he. Newman and Ruskin were as serious, elaborate, and even academic thinkers as he. But Ruskin let himself go about railways. Newman let himself go about Kingsley. Pater cannot let himself go for the excellent reason that he wants to stay: to stay at the point where all the keenest emotions meet, as he explains in the splendid peroration of *The Renaissance*. The only objection to being where all the keenest emotions meet is that you feel none of them.

In this sense Pater may well stand for a substantial summary of the æsthetes, apart from the purely poetical merits of men like Rossetti and Swinburne. Like Swinburne and others he first attempted to use mediæval tradition without trusting it. These people wanted to see Paganism *through* Christianity: because it involved the incidental amusement of seeing through Christianity itself. They not only tried to be in all ages at once (which is a very reasonable ambition, though not often realised), but they wanted to be on all sides at once: which is nonsense. Swinburne tries to question the philosophy of Christianity in the metres of a Christmas carol: and Dante Rossetti tries to write as if he were Christina Rossetti. Certainly the almost successful summit of all this attempt is Pater's superb passage on the Mona Lisa; in which he seeks to make her at once a mystery of good and a mystery of evil. The philosophy is false; even evidently false, for it bears no fruit to-day. There never was a woman, not Eve herself in the instant of temptation, who could smile the same smile as the mother of Helen and the mother of Mary. But it is the high-water mark of that vast attempt at an impartiality reached through art: and no other mere artist ever rose so high again.

Apart from this Ruskinian offshoot through Pre-Raphaelitism into what was called Æstheticism, the remains of the inspiration of Carlyle fill a very large part in the Victorian life, but not strictly so large a part in the Victorian literature. Charles Kingsley was a great publicist; a popular preacher; a popular novelist; and (in two cases at least) a very good novelist. His *Water Babies* is really a breezy and roaring freak; like a holiday at the seaside—a holiday where one talks natural history without taking it seriously. Some of the songs in this and other of his works are very real songs: notably, "When all the World is Young, Lad," which comes very near to being the only true defence of marriage in the controversies of the nineteenth century. But when all this is allowed, no one will seriously rank Kingsley, in the really literary sense, on the level of Carlyle or Ruskin, Tennyson or Browning, Dickens or Thackeray: and if such a place cannot be given to him, it can be given even less to his lusty and pleasant friend, Tom Hughes, whose personality floats towards the frankness of the *Boy's Own Paper*; or to his deep, suggestive metaphysical friend Maurice, who floats rather towards *The Hibbert Journal*. The moral and social influence of these things is not to be forgotten: but they leave the domain of letters. The voice of Carlyle is not heard again in letters till the coming of Kipling and Henley.

One other name of great importance should appear here, because it cannot appear very appropriately anywhere else: the man hardly belonged to the same school as Ruskin and Carlyle, but fought many of their battles, and was even more concentrated on their main task—the task of convicting liberal *bourgeois* England of priggishness and provinciality. I mean, of course, Matthew Arnold. Against Mill's "liberty" and Carlyle's "strength" and Ruskin's "nature," he set up a new presence and entity which he called "culture," the disinterested play of the mind through the sifting of the best books and authorities. Though a little dandified in phrase, he was undoubtedly serious and public-spirited in intention. He sometimes talked of culture almost as if it were a man, or at least a church (for a church has a sort of personality): some may suspect that culture was a man, whose name was Matthew Arnold. But Arnold was not only right but highly valuable. If we have said that Carlyle was a man that saw things, we may add that Arnold was chiefly valuable as a man who knew things. Well as he was endowed intellectually, his power came more from information than intellect. He simply happened to know certain things, that Carlyle didn't know, that Kingsley didn't know, that Huxley and Herbert Spencer didn't know: that England didn't know. He knew that England was a part of Europe: and not so important a part as it had been the morning after Waterloo. He knew that England was then (as it is now) an oligarchical State, and that many great nations are not. He knew that a real democracy need not live and does not live in that perpetual panic about using the powers of the State, which possessed men like Spencer and Cobden. He knew a rational minimum of culture and common courtesy could exist and did exist throughout large democracies. He knew the Catholic Church had been in history "the Church of the multitude": he knew it was not a sect. He knew that great landlords are no more a part of the economic law than nigger-drivers: he knew that small owners could and did prosper. He was not so much the philosopher as the man of the world: he reminded us that Europe was a society while Ruskin was treating it as a picture gallery. He was a sort of Heaven-sent courier. His frontal attack on the vulgar and sullen optimism of Victorian utility may be summoned up in the admirable sentence, in which he asked the English what was the use of a train taking them quickly from Islington to Camberwell, if it only took them "from a dismal and illiberal life in Islington to a dismal and illiberal life in Camberwell?"

His attitude to that great religious enigma round which all these great men were grouped as in a ring, was individual and decidedly curious. He seems to have believed that a "Historic Church," that is, some established organisation with ceremonies and sacred books, etc., could be perpetually preserved as a sort of vessel to contain the spiritual ideas of the age, whatever those ideas might happen to be. He clearly seems to have contemplated a melting away of the doctrines of the Church and even of the meaning of the words: but he thought a certain need in man would always be best satisfied by public worship and especially by the great religious literatures of the past. He would embalm the body that it might often be revisited by the soul—or souls. Something of the sort has been suggested by Dr. Coit and others of the ethical societies in our own time. But while Arnold would loosen the theological bonds of the Church, he would not loosen the official bonds of the State. You must not disestablish the Church: you must not even leave the Church: you must stop inside it and think what you choose. Enemies might say that he was simply trying to establish and endow Agnosticism. It is fairer and truer to say that unconsciously he was trying to restore Paganism: for this State Ritualism without theology, and without much belief, actually was the practice of the ancient world. Arnold may have thought that he was building an altar to the Unknown God; but he was really building it to Divus Cæsar.

As a critic he was chiefly concerned to preserve criticism itself; to set a measure to praise and blame and support the classics against the fashions. It is here that it is specially true of him, if of no writer else, that the style was the man. The most vital thing he invented was a new style: founded on the patient unravelling of the tangled Victorian ideas, as if they were matted hair under a comb. He did not mind how elaborately long he made a sentence, so long as he made it clear.

He would constantly repeat whole phrases word for word in the same sentence, rather than risk ambiguity by abbreviation. His genius showed itself in turning this method of a laborious lucidity into a peculiarly exasperating form of satire and controversy. Newman's strength was in a sort of stifled passion, a dangerous patience of polite logic and then: "Cowards! if I advanced a step you would run away: it is not you I fear. *Di me terrent, et Jupiter hostis.*" If Newman seemed suddenly to fly into a temper, Carlyle seemed never to fly out of one. But Arnold kept a smile of heart-broken forbearance, as of the teacher in an idiot school, that was enormously insulting. One trick he often tried with success. If his opponent had said something foolish, like "the destiny of England is in the great heart of England," Arnold would repeat the phrase again and again until it looked more foolish than it really was. Thus he recurs again and again to "the British College of Health in the New Road" till the reader wants to rush out and burn the place down. Arnold's great error was that he sometimes thus wearied us of his own phrases, as well as of his enemies'.

These names are roughly representative of the long series of protests against the cold commercial rationalism which held Parliament and the schools through the earlier Victorian time, in so far as those protests were made in the name of neglected intellect, insulted art, forgotten heroism and desecrated religion. But already the Utilitarian citadel had been more heavily bombarded on the other side by one lonely and unlettered man of genius.

The rise of Dickens is like the rising of a vast mob. This is not only because his tales are indeed as crowded and populous as towns: for truly it was not so much that Dickens appeared as that a hundred Dickens characters appeared. It is also because he was the sort of man who has the impersonal impetus of a mob: what Poe meant when he truly said that popular rumour, if really spontaneous, was like the intuition of the individual man of genius. Those who speak scornfully of the ignorance of the mob do not err as to the fact itself; their error is in not seeing that just as a crowd is comparatively ignorant, so a crowd is comparatively innocent. It will have the old and human faults; but it is not likely to specialise in the special faults of that particular society: because the effort of the strong and successful in all ages is to keep the poor out of society. If the higher castes have developed some special moral beauty or grace, as they occasionally do (for instance, mediæval chivalry), it is likely enough, of course, that the mass of men will miss it. But if they have developed some perversion or over-emphasis, as they much more often do (for instance, the Renaissance poisoning), then it will be the tendency of the mass of men to miss that too. The point might be put in many ways; you may say if you will that the poor are always at the tail of the procession, and that whether they are morally worse or better depends on whether humanity as a whole is proceeding towards heaven or hell. When humanity is going to hell, the poor are always nearest to heaven.

Dickens was a mob—and a mob in revolt; he fought by the light of nature; he had not a theory, but a thirst. If any one chooses to offer the cheap sarcasm that his thirst was largely a thirst for milk-punch, I am content to reply with complete gravity and entire contempt that in a sense this is perfectly true. His thirst was for things as humble, as human, as laughable as that daily bread for which we cry to God. He had no particular plan of reform; or, when he had, it was startlingly petty and parochial compared with the deep, confused clamour of comradeship and insurrection that fills all his narrative. It would not be gravely unjust to him to compare him to his own heroine, Arabella Allen, who "didn't know what she did like," but who (when confronted with Mr. Bob Sawyer) "did know what she didn't like." Dickens did know what he didn't like. He didn't like the Unrivalled Happiness which Mr. Roebuck praised; the economic laws that were working so faultlessly in Fever Alley; the wealth that was accumulating so rapidly in Bleeding Heart Yard. But, above all, he didn't like the *mean* side of the Manchester philosophy: the preaching of an impossible thrift and an intolerable temperance. He hated the implication that because a man was a miser in Latin he must also be a miser in English. And this meanness of the Utilitarians had gone very far—infecting many finer minds who had fought the Utilitarians. In the *Edinburgh Review*, a thing like Malthus could be championed by a man like Macaulay.

The twin root facts of the revolution called Dickens are these: first, that he attacked the cold Victorian compromise; second, that he attacked it without knowing he was doing it—certainly without knowing that other people were doing it. He was attacking something which we will call Mr. Gradgrind. He was utterly unaware (in any essential sense) that any one else had attacked Mr. Gradgrind. All the other attacks had come from positions of learning or cultured eccentricity of which he was entirely ignorant, and to which, therefore (like a spirited fellow), he felt a furious hostility. Thus, for instance, he hated that Little Bethel to which Kit's mother went: he hated it simply as Kit hated it. Newman could have told him it was hateful, because it had no root in religious history; it was not even a sapling sprung of the seed of some great human and heathen tree: it was a monstrous mushroom that grows in the moonshine and dies in the dawn. Dickens knew no more of religious history than Kit; he simply smelt the fungus, and it stank. Thus, again, he hated that insolent luxury of a class counting itself a comfortable exception to all mankind; he hated it as Kate Nickleby hated Sir Mulberry Hawke—by instinct. Carlyle could have told him that all the world was full of that anger against the impudent fatness of the few. But when Dickens wrote about Kate Nickleby, he knew about as much of the world—as Kate Nickleby. He did write *The Tale of Two Cities* long afterwards; but that was when he *had* been instructed by Carlyle. His first revolutionism was as private and internal as feeling sea-sick. Thus, once more, he wrote against Mr. Gradgrind long before he created him. In *The Chimes*, conceived in quite his casual and charitable season, with the *Christmas Carol* and the *Cricket on the Hearth*, he hit hard at the economists. Ruskin, in the same fashion, would have told him that the worst thing about the economists was that they were not economists: that they missed many essential things even in economics. But Dickens did not know whether they were economists or not: he only knew that they wanted hitting. Thus, to take a last case out of many, Dickens travelled in a French railway train, and noticed that this eccentric nation provided him with wine that he could drink and sandwiches he could eat, and manners he could tolerate. And remembering the ghastly sawdust-eating waiting-rooms of the North English railways, he wrote that rich chapter in *Mugby Junction*. Matthew Arnold could have told him that this was but a part of the general thinning down of European civilisation in these islands at the edge of it; that for two or three thousand years the Latin society has learnt how to drink wine, and how not to drink too much of it. Dickens did not in the least understand the Latin society: but he did understand the wine. If (to prolong an idle but not entirely false metaphor) we have called Carlyle a man who saw and Arnold a man who knew, we might truly call Dickens a man who tasted, that is, a man who really felt. In spite of all the silly talk about his vulgarity, he really had, in the strict and serious sense, good taste. All real good taste is gusto—the power of appreciating the presence—or the absence—of a particular and positive pleasure. He had no learning; he was not misled by the label on the bottle—for that is what learning largely meant in his time. He opened his mouth and shut his eyes and saw what the Age of Reason would give him. And, having tasted it, he spat it out.

I am constrained to consider Dickens here among the fighters; though I ought (on the pure principles of Art) to be considering him in the chapter which I have allotted to the story-tellers. But we should get the whole Victorian perspective wrong, in my opinion at least, if we did not see that Dickens was primarily the most successful of all the onslaughts on the solid scientific school; because he did not attack from the standpoint of extraordinary faith, like Newman; or the standpoint of extraordinary inspiration, like Carlyle; or the standpoint of extraordinary detachment or serenity, like Arnold; but from the standpoint of quite ordinary and quite hearty dislike. To give but one instance more, Matthew Arnold, trying to carry into England constructive educational schemes which he could see spread like a clear railway map all over the Continent, was much badgered about what he really thought was *wrong* with English middle-class education. Despairing of explaining to the English middle class the idea of high and central public instruction, as distinct from coarse and hole-and-corner private instruction, he invoked the aid of Dickens. He said the English middle-class school was the sort of school where Mr. Creakle sat, with his buttered toast and his cane. Now Dickens had probably never seen any other kind of school—certainly he had never understood the systematic State Schools in which Arnold had learnt his lesson. But he saw the cane and the buttered toast, and he *knew* that it was all wrong. In this sense, Dickens, the great romanticist, is truly the great realist also. For he had no abstractions: he had nothing except realities out of which to make a romance.

With Dickens, then, re-arises that reality with which I began and which (curtly, but I think not falsely) I have called Cobbett. In dealing with fiction as such, I shall have occasion to say wherein Dickens is weaker and stronger than that England of the eighteenth century: here it is sufficient to say that he represents the return of Cobbett in this vital sense; that he is proud of being the ordinary man. No one can understand the thousand caricatures by Dickens who does not understand that he is comparing them all with his own common sense. Dickens, in the bulk, liked the things that Cobbett had liked; what is perhaps more to the point, he hated the things that Cobbett had hated; the Tudors, the lawyers, the leisurely oppression of the poor. Cobbett's fine fighting journalism had been what is nowadays called "personal," that is, it supposed human beings to be human. But Cobbett was also personal in the less satisfactory sense; he could only multiply monsters who were exaggerations of his enemies or exaggerations of himself. Dickens was personal in a more godlike sense; he could multiply persons. He could create all the farce and tragedy of his age over again, with creatures unborn to sin and creatures unborn to suffer. That which had not been achieved by the fierce facts of Cobbett, the burning dreams of Carlyle, the white-hot proofs of Newman, was really or very nearly achieved by a crowd of impossible people. In the centre stood that citadel of atheist industrialism: and if indeed it has ever been taken, it was taken by the rush of that unreal army.

CHAPTER II

THE GREAT VICTORIAN NOVELISTS

The Victorian novel was a thing entirely Victorian; quite unique and suited to a sort of cosiness in that country and that age. But the novel itself, though not merely Victorian, is mainly modern. No clear-headed person wastes his time over definitions, except where he thinks his own definition would probably be in dispute. I merely say, therefore, that when I say "novel," I mean a fictitious narrative (almost invariably, but not necessarily, in prose) of which the essential is that the story is not told for the sake of its naked pointedness as an anecdote, or for the sake of the irrelevant landscapes and visions that can be caught up in it, but for the sake of some study of the difference between human beings. There are several things that make this mode of art unique. One of the most conspicuous is that it is the art in which the conquests of woman are quite beyond controversy. The proposition that Victorian women have done well in politics and philosophy is not necessarily an untrue proposition; but it is a partisan proposition. I never heard that many women, let alone men, shared the views of Mary Wollstonecraft; I never heard that millions of believers flocked to the religion tentatively founded by Miss Frances Power Cobbe. They did, undoubtedly, flock to Mrs. Eddy; but it will not be unfair to that lady to call her following a sect, and not altogether unreasonable to say that such insane exceptions prove the rule. Nor can I at this moment think of a single modern woman writing on politics or abstract things, whose work is of undisputed importance; except perhaps Mrs. Sidney Webb, who settles things by the simple process of ordering about the citizens of a state, as she might the servants in a kitchen. There has been, at any rate, no writer on moral or political theory that can be mentioned, without seeming comic, in the same breath with the great female novelists. But when we come to the novelists, the women have, on the whole, equality; and certainly, in some points, superiority. Jane Austen is as strong in her own way as Scott is in his. But she is, for all practical purposes, never weak in her own way—and Scott very often is. Charlotte Brontë dedicated *Jane Eyre* to the author of *Vanity Fair*. I should hesitate to say that Charlotte Brontë's is a better book than Thackeray's, but I think it might well be maintained that it is a better story. All sorts of inquiring asses (equally ignorant of the old nature of woman and the new nature of the novel) whispered wisely that George Eliot's novels were really written by George Lewes. I will cheerfully answer for the fact that, if they had been written by George Lewes, no one would ever have read them. Those who have read his book on Robespierre will have no doubt about my meaning. I am no idolater of George Eliot; but a man who could concoct such a crushing opiate about the most exciting occasion in history certainly did not write *The Mill on the Floss*. This is the first fact about the novel, that it is the introduction of a new and rather curious kind of art; and it has been found to be peculiarly feminine, from the first good novel by Fanny Burney to the last good novel by Miss May Sinclair. The truth is, I think, that the modern novel is a new thing; not new in its essence (for that is a philosophy for fools), but new in the sense that it lets loose many of the things that are old. It is a hearty and exhaustive overhauling of that part of human existence which has always been the woman's province, or rather kingdom; the play of personalities in private, the real difference between Tommy and Joe. It is right that womanhood should specialise in individuals, and be praised for doing so; just as in the Middle Ages she specialised in dignity and was praised for doing so. People put the matter wrong when they say that the novel is a study of human nature. Human nature is a thing that even men can understand. Human nature is born of the pain of a woman; human nature plays at peep-bo when it is two and at cricket when it is twelve; human nature earns its living and desires the other sex and dies. What the novel deals with is what women have to deal with; the differentiations, the twists and turns of this eternal river. The key of this new form of art, which we call fiction, is sympathy. And sympathy does not mean so much feeling with all who feel, but rather suffering with all who suffer. And it was inevitable, under such an inspiration, that more attention should be given to the awkward corners of life than to its even flow. The very promising domestic channel dug by the Victorian women, in books like *Cranford*, by Mrs. Gaskell, would have got to the sea, if they had been left alone to dig it. They might have made domesticity a fairyland. Unfortunately another idea, the idea of imitating men's cuffs and collars and documents, cut across this purely female discovery and destroyed it.

It may seem mere praise of the novel to say it is the art of sympathy and the study of human variations. But indeed, though this is a good thing, it is not universally good. We have gained in sympathy; but we have lost in brotherhood. Old quarrels had more equality than modern exonerations. Two peasants in the Middle Ages quarrelled about their two fields. But they went to the same church, served in the same semi-feudal militia, and had the same morality, which ever might happen to be breaking it at the moment. The very cause of their quarrel was the cause of their fraternity; they both liked land. But suppose one of them a teetotaler who desired the abolition of hops on both farms; suppose the other a vegetarian who desired the abolition of chickens on both farms: and it is at once apparent that a quarrel of quite a different kind would begin; and that in that quarrel it would not be a question of farmer against farmer, but of individual against individual. This fundamental sense of human fraternity can only exist in the presence of positive religion. Man is merely man only when he is seen against the sky. If he is seen against any landscape, he is only a man of that land. If he is seen against any house, he is only a householder. Only where death and eternity are intensely present can human beings fully feel their fellowship. Once the divine darkness against which we stand is really dismissed from the mind (as it was very nearly dismissed in the Victorian time) the differences between human beings become overpoweringly plain; whether they are expressed in the high caricatures of Dickens or the low lunacies of Zola.

This can be seen in a sort of picture in the Prologue of the *Canterbury Tales*; which is already pregnant with the promise of the English novel. The characters there are at once graphically and delicately differentiated; the Doctor with his rich cloak, his careful meals, his coldness to religion; the Franklin, whose white beard was so fresh that it recalled the daisies, and in whose house it snowed meat and drink; the Summoner, from whose fearful face, like a red cherub's, the children fled, and who wore a garland like a hoop; the Miller with his short red hair and bagpipes and brutal head, with which he could break down a door; the Lover who was as sleepless as a nightingale; the Knight, the Cook, the Clerk of Oxford. Pendennis or the Cook, M. Mirabolant, is nowhere so vividly varied by a few merely verbal strokes. But the great difference is deeper and more striking. It is simply that Pendennis would never have gone riding with a cook at all. Chaucer's knight rode with a cook quite naturally; because the thing they were all seeking together was as much above knighthood as it was above cookery. Soldiers and swindlers and bullies and outcasts, they were all going to the shrine of a distant saint. To what sort of distant saint would Pendennis and Colonel Newcome and Mr. Moss and Captain Costigan and Ridley the butler and Bayham and Sir Barnes Newcome and Laura and the Duchess d'Ivry and Warrington and Captain Blackball and Lady Kew travel, laughing and telling tales together?

The growth of the novel, therefore, must not be too easily called an increase in the interest in humanity. It is an increase in the interest in the things in which men differ; much fuller and finer work had been done before about the things in which they agree. And this intense interest in variety had its bad side as well as its good; it has rather increased social distinctions in a serious and spiritual sense. Most of the oblivion of democracy is due to the oblivion of death. But in its own manner and measure, it was a real advance and experiment of the European mind, like the public art of the Renaissance or the fairyland of physical science explored in the nineteenth century. It was a more unquestionable benefit than these: and in that development women played a peculiar part, English women especially, and Victorian women most of all.

It is perhaps partly, though certainly not entirely, this influence of the great women writers that explains another very arresting and important fact about the emergence of genuinely Victorian fiction. It had been by this time decided, by the powers that had influence (and by public opinion also, at least in the middle-class sense), that certain verbal limits must be set to such literature. The novel must be what some would call pure and others would call prudish; but what is not, properly considered, either one or the other: it is rather a more or less business proposal (right or wrong) that every writer shall draw the line at literal physical description of things socially concealed. It was originally merely verbal; it had not, primarily, any dream of purifying the topic or the moral tone. Dickens and Thackeray claimed very properly the right to deal with shameful passions and suggest their shameful culminations; Scott sometimes dealt with ideas positively horrible—as in that grand Glenallan tragedy which is as appalling as the *Œdipus* or *The Cenci*. None of these great men would have tolerated for a moment being talked to (as the muddle-headed amateur censors talk to artists to-day) about "wholesome" topics and suggestions "that cannot elevate." They had to describe the great battle of good and evil and they described both; but they accepted a working Victorian compromise about what should happen behind the scenes and what on the stage. Dickens did not claim the license of diction Fielding might have claimed in repeating the senile ecstasies of Gride (let us say) over his purchased bride: but Dickens does not leave the reader in the faintest doubt about what sort of feelings they were; nor is there any reason why he should. Thackeray would not have described the toilet details of the secret balls of Lord Steyne: he left that to Lady Cardigan. But no one who had read Thackeray's version would be surprised at Lady Cardigan's. But though the great Victorian novelists would not have permitted the impudence of the suggestion that every part of their problem must be wholesome and innocent in itself, it is still tenable (I do not say it is certain) that by yielding to the Philistines on this verbal compromise, they have in the long run worked for impurity rather than purity. In one point I do certainly think that Victorian Bowdlerism did pure harm. This is the simple point that, nine times out of ten, the coarse word is the word that condemns an evil and the refined word the word that excuses it. A common evasion, for instance, substitutes for the word that brands self-sale as the essential sin, a word which weakly suggests that it is no more wicked than walking down the street. The great peril of such soft mystifications is that extreme evils (they that are abnormal even by the standard of evil) have a very long start. Where ordinary wrong is made unintelligible, extraordinary wrong can count on remaining more unintelligible still; especially among those who live in such an atmosphere of long words. It is a cruel comment on the purity of the Victorian Age, that the age ended (save for the bursting of a single scandal) in a thing being everywhere called "Art," "The Greek Spirit," "The Platonic Ideal" and so on—which any navvy mending the road outside would have stamped with a word as vile and as vulgar as it deserved.

This reticence, right or wrong, may have been connected with the participation of women with men in the matter of fiction. It is an important point: the sexes can only be coarse separately. It was certainly also due, as I have already suggested, to the treaty between the rich *bourgeoisie* and the old aristocracy, which both had to make, for the common and congenial purpose of keeping the English people down. But it was due much more than this to a general moral atmosphere in the Victorian Age. It is impossible to express that spirit except by the electric bell of a name. It was latitudinarian, and yet it was limited. It could be content with nothing less than the whole cosmos: yet the cosmos with which it was content was small. It is false to say it was without humour: yet there was something by instinct unsmiling in it. It was always saying solidly that things were "enough"; and proving by that sharpness (as of the shutting of a door) that they were not enough. It took, I will not say its pleasures, but even its emancipations, sadly. Definitions seem to escape this way and that in the attempt to locate it as an idea. But every one will understand me if I call it George Eliot.

I begin with this great woman of letters for both the two reasons already mentioned. She represents the rationalism of the old Victorian Age at its highest. She and Mill are like two great mountains at the end of that long, hard chain which is the watershed of the Early Victorian time. They alone rise high enough to be confused among the clouds—or perhaps confused among the stars. They certainly were seeking truth, as Newman and Carlyle were; the slow slope of the later Victorian vulgarity does not lower their precipice and pinnacle. But I begin with this name also because it emphasises the idea of modern fiction as a fresh and largely a female thing. The novel of the nineteenth century was female; as fully as the novel of the eighteenth century was male. It is quite certain that no woman could have written *Roderick Random*. It is not quite so certain that no woman could have written *Esmond*. The strength and subtlety of woman had certainly sunk deep into English letters when George Eliot began to write.

Her originals and even her contemporaries had shown the feminine power in fiction as well or better than she. Charlotte Brontë, understood along her own instincts, was as great; Jane Austen was greater. The latter comes into our present consideration only as that most exasperating thing, an ideal unachieved. It is like leaving an unconquered fortress in the rear. No woman later has captured the complete common sense of Jane Austen. She could keep her head, while all the after women went about looking for their brains. She could describe a man coolly; which neither George Eliot nor Charlotte Brontë could do. She knew what she knew, like a sound dogmatist: she did not know what she did not know—like a sound agnostic. But she belongs to a vanished world before the great progressive age of which I write.

One of the characteristics of the central Victorian spirit was a tendency to substitute a certain more or less satisfied seriousness for the extremes of tragedy and comedy. This is marked by a certain change in George Eliot; as it is marked by a certain limitation or moderation in Dickens. Dickens was the People, as it was in the eighteenth century and still largely is, in spite of all the talk for and against Board School Education: comic, tragic, realistic, free-spoken, far looser in words than in deeds. It marks the silent strength and pressure of the spirit of the Victorian middle class that even to Dickens it never occurred to revive the verbal coarseness of Smollett or Swift. The other proof of the same pressure is the change in George Eliot. She was not a genius in the elemental sense of Dickens; she could never have been either so strong or so soft. But she did originally represent some of the same popular realities: and her first books (at least as compared with her latest) were full of sound fun and bitter pathos. Mr. Max Beerbohm has remarked (in his glorious essay called *Ichabod*, I think), that Silas Marner would not have forgotten his miserliness if George Eliot had written of him in her maturity. I have a great regard for Mr. Beerbohm's literary judgments; and it may be so. But if literature means anything more than a cold calculation of the chances, if there is in it, as I believe, any deeper idea of detaching the spirit of life from the dull obstacles of life, of permitting human nature really to reveal itself as human, if (to put it shortly) literature has anything on earth to do with being *interesting*—then I think we would rather have a few more Marners than that rich maturity that gave us the analysed dust-heaps of *Daniel Deronda*.

In her best novels there is real humour, of a cool sparkling sort; there is a strong sense of substantial character that has not yet degenerated into psychology; there is a great deal of wisdom, chiefly about women; indeed there is almost every element of literature except a certain indescribable thing called *glamour*; which was the whole stock-in-trade of the Brontës, which we feel in Dickens when Quilp clambers amid rotten wood by the desolate river; and even in Thackeray when Esmond with his melancholy eyes wanders like some swarthy crow about the dismal avenues of Castlewood. Of this quality (which some have called, but hastily, the essential of literature) George Eliot had not little but nothing. Her air is bright and intellectually even exciting; but it is like the air of a cloudless day on the parade at Brighton. She sees people clearly, but not through an atmosphere. And she can conjure up storms in the conscious, but not in the subconscious mind.

It is true (though the idea should not be exaggerated) that this deficiency was largely due to her being cut off from all those conceptions that had made the fiction of a Muse; the deep idea that there are really demons and angels behind men. Certainly the increasing atheism of her school spoilt her own particular imaginative talent: she was far less free when she thought like Ladislaw than when she thought like Casaubon. It also betrayed her on a matter specially requiring common sense; I mean sex. There is nothing that is so profoundly false as rationalist flirtation. Each sex is trying to be both sexes at once; and the result is a confusion more untruthful than any conventions. This can easily be seen by comparing her with a greater woman who died before the beginning of our present problem. Jane Austen was born before those bonds which (we are told) protected woman from truth, were burst by the Brontës or elaborately untied by George Eliot. Yet the fact remains that Jane Austen knew much more about men than either of them. Jane Austen may have been protected from truth: but it was precious little of truth that was protected from her. When Darcy, in finally confessing his faults, says, "I have been a selfish being all my life, in practice *though not in theory*," he gets nearer to a complete confession of the intelligent male than ever was even hinted by the Byronic lapses of the Brontës' heroes or the elaborate exculpations of George Eliot's. Jane Austen, of course, covered an infinitely smaller field than any of her later rivals; but I have always believed in the victory of small nationalities.

The Brontës suggest themselves here; because their superficial qualities, the qualities that can be seized upon in satire, were in this an exaggeration of what was, in George Eliot, hardly more than an omission. There was perhaps a time when Mr. Rawjester was more widely known than Mr. Rochester. And certainly Mr. Rochester (to adopt the diction of that other eminent country gentleman, Mr. Darcy) was simply individualistic not only in practice, but in theory. Now any one may be so in practice: but a man who is simply individualistic in theory must merely be an ass. Undoubtedly the Brontës exposed themselves to some misunderstanding by thus perpetually making the masculine creature much more masculine than he wants to be. Thackeray (a man of strong though sleepy virility) asked in his exquisite plaintive way: "Why do our lady novelists make the men bully the women?" It is, I think, unquestionably true that the Brontës treated the male as an almost anarchic thing coming in from outside nature; much as people on this planet regard a comet. Even the really delicate and sustained comedy of Paul Emanuel is not quite free from this air of studying something alien. The reply may be made that the women in men's novels are equally fallacious. The reply is probably just.

What the Brontës really brought into fiction was exactly what Carlyle brought into history; the blast of the mysticism of the North. They were of Irish blood settled on the windy heights of Yorkshire; in that country where Catholicism lingered latest, but in a superstitious form; where modern industrialism came earliest and was more superstitious still. The strong winds and sterile places, the old tyranny of barons and the new and blacker tyranny of manufacturers, has made and left that country a land of barbarians. All Charlotte Brontë's earlier work is full of that sullen and unmanageable world; moss-troopers turned hurriedly into miners; the last of the old world forced into supporting the very first crudities of the new. In this way Charlotte Brontë represents the Victorian settlement in a special way. The Early Victorian Industrialism is to George Eliot and to Charlotte Brontë, rather as the Late Victorian Imperialism would have been to Mrs. Humphry Ward in the centre of the empire and to Miss Olive Schreiner at the edge of it. The real strength there is in characters like Robert Moore, when he is dealing with anything except women, is the romance of industry in its first advance: a romance that has not remained. On such fighting frontiers people always exaggerate the strong qualities the masculine sex does possess, and always add a great many strong qualities that it does not possess. That is, briefly, all the reason in the Brontës on this special subject: the rest is stark unreason. It can be most clearly seen in that sister of Charlotte Brontë's who has achieved the real feat of remaining as a great woman rather than a great writer. There is really, in a narrow but intense way, a tradition of Emily Brontë: as there is a tradition of St. Peter or Dr. Johnson. People talk as if they had known her, apart from her works. She must have been something more than an original person; perhaps an origin. But so far as her written works go she enters English letters only as an original person—and rather a narrow one. Her imagination was sometimes superhuman—always inhuman. *Wuthering Heights* might have been written by an eagle. She is the strongest instance of these strong imaginations that made the other sex a monster: for Heathcliffe fails as a man as catastrophically as he succeeds as a demon. I think Emily Brontë was further narrowed by the broadness of her religious views; but never, of course, so much as George Eliot.

In any case, it is Charlotte Brontë who enters Victorian literature. The shortest way of stating her strong contribution is, I think, this: that she reached the highest romance through the lowest realism. She did not set out with Amadis of Gaul in a forest or with Mr. Pickwick in a comic club. She set out with herself, with her own dingy clothes, and accidental ugliness, and flat, coarse, provincial household; and forcibly fused all such muddy materials into a spirited fairy-tale. If the first chapters on the home and school had not proved how heavy and hateful *sanity* can be, there would really be less point in the insanity of Mr. Rochester's wife—or the not much milder insanity of Mrs. Rochester's husband. She discovered the secret of hiding the sensational in the commonplace: and *Jane Eyre* remains the best of her books (better even than *Villette*) because while it is a human document written in blood, it is also one of the best blood-and-thunder detective stories in the world.

But while Emily Brontë was as unsociable as a storm at midnight, and while Charlotte Brontë was at best like that warmer and more domestic thing, a house on fire—they do connect themselves with the calm of George Eliot, as the forerunners of many later developments of the feminine advance. Many forerunners (if it comes to that) would have felt rather ill if they had seen the things they foreran. This notion of a hazy anticipation of after history has been absurdly overdone: as when men connect Chaucer with the Reformation; which is like connecting Homer with the Syracusan Expedition. But it is to some extent true that all these great Victorian women had a sort of unrest in their souls. And the proof of it is that (after what I will claim to call the healthier time of Dickens and Thackeray) it began to be admitted by the great Victorian men. If there had not been something in that irritation, we should hardly have had to speak in these pages of *Diana of the Crossways* or of *Tess of the D'Urbervilles*. To what this strange and very local sex war has been due I shall not ask, because I have no answer. That it was due to votes or even little legal inequalities about marriage, I feel myself here too close to realities even to discuss. My own guess is that it has been due to the great neglect of the military spirit by the male Victorians. The woman felt obscurely that she was still running her mortal risk, while the man was not still running his. But I know nothing about it; nor does anybody else.

In so short a book on so vast, complex and living a subject, it is impossible to drop even into the second rank of good authors, whose name is legion; but it is impossible to leave that considerable female force in fiction which has so largely made the very nature of the modern novel, without mentioning two names which almost brought that second rank up to the first rank. They were at utterly opposite poles. The one succeeded by being a much mellower and more Christian George Eliot; the other succeeded by being a much more mad and unchristian Emily Brontë. But Mrs. Oliphant and the author calling herself "Ouida" both forced themselves well within the frontier of fine literature. *The Beleaguered City* is literature in its highest sense; the other works of its author tend to fall into fiction in its best working sense. Mrs. Oliphant was infinitely saner in that city of ghosts than the cosmopolitan Ouida ever was in any of the cities of men. Mrs. Oliphant would never have dared to discover, either in heaven or hell, such a thing as a hairbrush with its back encrusted with diamonds. But though Ouida was violent and weak where Mrs. Oliphant might have been mild and strong, her own triumphs were her own. She had a real power of expressing the senses through her style; of conveying the very heat of blue skies or the bursting of palpable pomegranates. And just as Mrs. Oliphant transfused her more timid Victorian tales with a true and intense faith in the Christian mystery—so Ouida, with infinite fury and infinite confusion of thought, did fill her books with Byron and the remains of the French Revolution. In the track of such genius there has been quite an accumulation of true talent as in the children's tales of Mrs. Ewing, the historical tales of Miss Yonge, the tales of Mrs. Molesworth, and so on. On a general review I do not think I have been wrong in taking the female novelists first. I think they gave its special shape, its temporary twist, to the Victorian novel.

Nevertheless it is a shock (I almost dare to call it a relief) to come back to the males. It is the more abrupt because the first name that must be mentioned derives directly from the mere maleness of the Sterne and Smollett novel. I have already spoken of Dickens as the most homely and instinctive, and therefore probably the heaviest, of all the onslaughts made on the central Victorian satisfaction. There is therefore the less to say of him here, where we consider him only as a novelist; but there is still much more to say than can even conceivably be said. Dickens, as we have stated, inherited the old comic, rambling novel from Smollett and the rest. Dickens, as we have also stated, consented to expurgate that novel. But when all origins and all restraints have been defined and allowed for, the creature that came out was such as we shall not see again. Smollett was coarse; but Smollett was also cruel. Dickens was frequently horrible; he was never cruel. The art of Dickens was the most exquisite of arts: it was the art of enjoying everybody. Dickens, being a very human writer, had to be a very human being; he had his faults and sensibilities in a strong degree; and I do not for a moment maintain that he enjoyed everybody in his daily life. But he enjoyed everybody in his books: and everybody has enjoyed everybody in those books even till to-day. His books are full of baffled villains stalking out or cowardly bullies kicked downstairs. But the villains and the cowards are such delightful people that the reader always hopes the villain will put his head through a side window and make a last remark; or that the bully will say one thing more, even from the bottom of the stairs. The reader really hopes this; and he cannot get rid of the fancy that the author hopes so too. I cannot at the moment recall that Dickens ever killed a comic villain, except Quilp, who was deliberately made even more villainous than comic. There can be no serious fears for the life of Mr. Wegg in the muckcart; though Mr. Pecksniff fell to be a borrower of money, and Mr. Mantalini to turning a mangle, the human race has the comfort of thinking they are still alive: and one might have the rapture of receiving a begging letter from Mr. Pecksniff, or even of catching Mr. Mantalini collecting the washing, if one always lurked about on Monday mornings. This sentiment (the true artist will be relieved to hear) is entirely unmoral. Mrs. Wilfer deserved death much more than Mr. Quilp, for she had succeeded in poisoning family life persistently, while he was (to say the least of it) intermittent in his domesticity. But who can honestly say he does not hope Mrs. Wilfer is still talking like Mrs. Wilfer—especially if it is only in a book? This is the artistic greatness of Dickens, before and after which there is really nothing to be said. He had the power of creating people, both possible and impossible, who were simply precious and priceless people; and anything subtler added to that truth really only weakens it.

The mention of Mrs. Wilfer (whom the heart is loth to leave) reminds one of the only elementary ethical truth that is essential in the study of Dickens. That is that he had broad or universal sympathies in a sense totally unknown to the social reformers who wallow in such phrases. Dickens (unlike the social reformers) really did sympathise with every sort of victim of every sort of tyrant. He did truly pray for *all* who are desolate and oppressed. If you try to tie him to any cause narrower than that Prayer Book definition, you will find you have shut out half his best work. If, in your sympathy for Mrs. Quilp, you call Dickens the champion of downtrodden woman, you will suddenly remember Mr. Wilfer, and find yourself unable to deny the existence of downtrodden man. If in your sympathy for Mr. Rouncewell you call Dickens the champion of a manly middle-class Liberalism against Chesney Wold, you will suddenly remember Stephen Blackpool—and find yourself unable to deny that Mr. Rouncewell might be a pretty insupportable cock on his own dung-hill. If in your sympathy for Stephen Blackpool you call Dickens a Socialist (as does Mr. Pugh), and think of him as merely heralding the great Collectivist revolt against Victorian Individualism and Capitalism, which seemed so clearly to be the crisis at the end of this epoch—you will suddenly remember the agreeable young Barnacle at the Circumlocution Office: and you will be unable, for very shame, to assert that Dickens would have trusted the poor to a State Department. Dickens did not merely believe in the brotherhood of men in the weak modern way; he was the brotherhood of men, and knew it was a brotherhood in sin as well as in aspiration. And he was not only larger than the old factions he satirised; he was larger than any of our great social schools that have gone forward since he died.

The seemingly quaint custom of comparing Dickens and Thackeray existed in their own time, and no one will dismiss it with entire disdain who remembers that the Victorian tradition was domestic and genuine, even when it was hoodwinked and unworldly. There must have been some reason for making this imaginary duel between two quite separate and quite amiable acquaintances. And there is, after all, some reason for it. It is not, as was once cheaply said, that Thackeray went in for truth, and Dickens for mere caricature. There is a huge accumulation of truth, down to the smallest detail, in Dickens: he seems sometimes a mere mountain of facts. Thackeray, in comparison, often seems quite careless and elusive; almost as if he did not quite know where all his characters were. There is a truth behind the popular distinction; but it lies much deeper. Perhaps the best way of stating it is this: that Dickens used reality, while aiming at an effect of romance; while Thackeray used the loose language and ordinary approaches of romance, while aiming at an effect of reality. It was the special and splendid business of Dickens to introduce us to people who would have been quite incredible if he had not told us so much truth about them. It was the special and not less splendid task of Thackeray to introduce us to people whom we knew already. Paradoxically, but very practically, it followed that his introductions were the longer of the two. When we hear of Aunt Betsy Trotwood, we vividly envisage everything about her, from her gardening gloves to her seaside residence, from her hard, handsome face to her tame lunatic laughing at the bedroom window. It is all so minutely true that she must be true also. We only feel inclined to walk round the English coast until we find that particular garden and that particular aunt. But when we turn from the aunt of Copperfield to the uncle of Pendennis, we are more likely to run round the coast trying to find a watering-place where he isn't than one where he is. The moment one sees Major Pendennis, one sees a hundred Major Pendennises. It is not a matter of mere realism. Miss Trotwood's bonnet and gardening tools and cupboard full of old-fashioned bottles are quite as true in the materialistic way as the Major's cuffs and corner table and toast and newspaper. Both writers are realistic: but Dickens writes realism in order to make the incredible credible. Thackeray writes it in order to make us recognise an old friend. Whether we shall be pleased to meet the old friend is quite another matter: I think we should be better pleased to meet Miss Trotwood, and find, as David Copperfield did, a new friend, a new world. But we recognise Major Pendennis even when we avoid him. Henceforth Thackeray can count on our seeing him from his wig to his well-blacked boots whenever he chooses to say "Major Pendennis paid a call." Dickens, on the other hand, had to keep up an incessant excitement about his characters; and no man on earth but he could have kept it up.

It may be said, in approximate summary, that Thackeray is the novelist of memory—of our memories as well as his own. Dickens seems to expect all his characters, like amusing strangers arriving at lunch: as if they gave him not only pleasure, but surprise. But Thackeray is everybody's past—is everybody's youth. Forgotten friends flit about the passages of dreamy colleges and unremembered clubs; we hear fragments of unfinished conversations, we see faces without names for an instant, fixed for ever in some trivial grimace: we smell the strong smell of social cliques now quite incongruous to us; and there stir in all the little rooms at once the hundred ghosts of oneself.

For this purpose Thackeray was equipped with a singularly easy and sympathetic style, carved in slow soft curves where Dickens hacked out his images with a hatchet. There was a sort of avuncular indulgence about his attitude; what he called his "preaching" was at worst a sort of grumbling, ending with the sentiment that boys will be boys and that there's nothing new under the sun. He was not really either a cynic or a *censor morum*; but (in another sense than Chaucer's) a gentle pardoner: having seen the weaknesses he is sometimes almost weak about them. He really comes nearer to exculpating Pendennis or Ethel Newcome than any other author, who saw what he saw, would have been. The rare wrath of such men is all the more effective; and there are passages in

Vanity Fair and still more in *The Book of Snobs*, where he does make the dance of wealth and fashion look stiff and monstrous, like a Babylonian masquerade. But he never quite did it in such a way as to turn the course of the Victorian Age.

It may seem strange to say that Thackeray did not know enough of the world; yet this was the truth about him in large matters of the philosophy of life, and especially of his own time. He did not know the way things were going: he was too Victorian to understand the Victorian epoch. He did not know enough ignorant people to have heard the news. In one of his delightful asides he imagines two little clerks commenting erroneously on the appearance of Lady Kew or Sir Brian Newcome in the Park, and says: "How should Jones and Brown, who are not, *vous comprenez, du monde*, understand these mysteries?" But I think Thackeray knew quite as little about Jones and Brown as they knew about Newcome and Kew; his world was *le monde*. Hence he seemed to take it for granted that the Victorian compromise would last; while Dickens (who knew his Jones and Brown) had already guessed that it would not. Thackeray did not realise that the Victorian platform was a moving platform. To take but one instance, he was a Radical like Dickens; all really representative Victorians, except perhaps Tennyson, were Radicals. But he seems to have thought of all reform as simple and straightforward and all of a piece; as if Catholic Emancipation, the New Poor Law, Free Trade and the Factory Acts and Popular Education were all parts of one almost self-evident evolution of enlightenment. Dickens, being in touch with the democracy, had already discovered that the country had come to a dark place of divided ways and divided counsels. In *Hard Times* he realised Democracy at war with Radicalism; and became, with so incompatible an ally as Ruskin, not indeed a Socialist, but certainly an anti-Individualist. In *Our Mutual Friend* he felt the strength of the new rich, and knew they had begun to transform the aristocracy, instead of the aristocracy transforming them. He knew that Veneering had carried off Twemlow in triumph. He very nearly knew what we all know to-day: that, so far from it being possible to plod along the progressive road with more votes and more Free Trade, England must either sharply become very much more democratic or as rapidly become very much less so.

There gathers round these two great novelists a considerable group of good novelists, who more or less mirror their mid-Victorian mood. Wilkie Collins may be said to be in this way a lesser Dickens and Anthony Trollope a lesser Thackeray. Wilkie Collins is chiefly typical of his time in this respect: that while his moral and religious conceptions were as mechanical as his carefully constructed fictitious conspiracies, he nevertheless informed the latter with a sort of involuntary mysticism which dealt wholly with the darker side of the soul. For this was one of the most peculiar of the problems of the Victorian mind. The idea of the supernatural was perhaps at as low an ebb as it had ever been—certainly much lower than it is now. But in spite of this, and in spite of a certain ethical cheeriness that was almost *de rigueur*—the strange fact remains that the only sort of supernaturalism the Victorians allowed to their imaginations was a sad supernaturalism. They might have ghost stories, but not saints' stories. They could trifle with the curse or unpardoning prophecy of a witch, but not with the pardon of a priest. They seem to have held (I believe erroneously) that the supernatural was safest when it came from below. When we think (for example) of the uncountable riches of religious art, imagery, ritual and popular legend that has clustered round Christmas through all the Christian ages, it is a truly extraordinary thing to reflect that Dickens (wishing to have in *The Christmas Carol* a little happy supernaturalism by way of a change) actually had to make up a mythology for himself. Here was one of the rare cases where Dickens, in a real and human sense, did suffer from the lack of culture. For the rest, Wilkie Collins is these two elements: the mechanical and the mystical; both very good of their kind. He is one of the few novelists in whose case it is proper and literal to speak of his "plots." He was a plotter; he went about to slay Godfrey Ablewhite as coldly and craftily as the Indians did. But he also had a sound though sinister note of true magic; as in the repetition of the two white dresses in *The Woman in White*; or of the dreams with their double explanations in *Armadale*. His ghosts do walk. They are alive; and walk as softly as Count Fosco, but as solidly. Finally, *The Moonstone* is probably the best detective tale in the world.

Anthony Trollope, a clear and very capable realist, represents rather another side of the Victorian spirit of comfort; its leisureliness, its love of detail, especially of domestic detail; its love of following characters and kindred from book to book and from generation to generation. Dickens very seldom tried this latter experiment, and then (as in *Master Humphrey's Clock*) unsuccessfully; those magnesium blazes of his were too brilliant and glaring to be indefinitely prolonged. But Thackeray was full of it; and we often feel that the characters in *The Newcomes* or *Philip* might legitimately complain that their talk and tale are being perpetually interrupted and pestered by people out of other books. Within his narrower limits, Trollope was a more strict and masterly realist than Thackeray, and even those who would call his personages "types" would admit that they are as vivid as characters. It was a bustling but a quiet world that he described: politics before the coming of the Irish and the Socialists; the Church in the lull between the Oxford Movement and the modern High Anglican energy. And it is notable in the Victorian spirit once more that though his clergymen are all of them real men and many of them good men, it never really occurs to us to think of them as the priests of a religion.

Charles Reade may be said to go along with these; and Disraeli and even Kingsley; not because these three very different persons had anything particular in common, but because they all fell short of the first rank in about the same degree. Charles Reade had a kind of cold coarseness about him, not morally but artistically, which keeps him out of the best literature as such: but he is of importance to the Victorian development in another way; because he has the harsher and more tragic note that has come later in the study of our social problems. He is the first of the angry realists. Kingsley's best books may be called boys' books. There is a real though a juvenile poetry in *Westward Ho!* and though that narrative, historically considered, is very much of a lie, it is a good, thundering honest lie. There are also genuinely eloquent things in *Hypatia*, and a certain electric atmosphere of sectarian excitement that Kingsley kept himself in, and did know how to convey. He said he wrote the book in his heart's blood. This is an exaggeration, but there is a truth in it; and one does feel that he may have relieved his feelings by writing it in red ink. As for Disraeli, his novels are able and interesting considered as everything except novels, and are an important contribution precisely because they are written by an alien who did not take our politics so seriously as Trollope did. They are important again as showing those later Victorian changes which men like Thackeray missed. Disraeli did do something towards revealing the dishonesty of our politics—even if he had done a good deal towards bringing it about.

Between this group and the next there hovers a figure very hard to place; not higher in letters than these, yet not easy to class with them; I mean Bulwer Lytton. He was no greater than they were; yet somehow he seems to take up more space. He did not, in the ultimate reckoning, do anything in particular: but he was a figure; rather as Oscar Wilde was later a figure. You could not have the Victorian Age without him. And this was not due to wholly superficial things like his dandyism, his dark, sinister good looks and a great deal of the mere polished melodrama that he wrote. There was something in his all-round interests; in the variety of things he tried; in his half-aristocratic swagger as poet and politician, that made him in some ways a real touchstone of the time. It is noticeable about him that he is always turning up everywhere and that he brings other people out, generally in a hostile spirit. His Byronic and almost Oriental ostentation was used by the young Thackeray as something on which to sharpen his new razor of Victorian common sense. His pose as a dilettante satirist inflamed the execrable temper of Tennyson, and led to those lively comparisons to a bandbox and a lion in curlpapers. He interposed the glove of warning and the tear of sensibility between us and the proper ending of *Great Expectations*. Of his own books, by far the best are the really charming comedies about *The Caxtons* and *Kenelm Chillingly*; none of his other works have a high literary importance now, with the possible exception of *A Strange Story*; but his *Coming Race* is historically interesting as foreshadowing those novels of the future which were afterwards such a weapon of the Socialists. Lastly, there was an element indefinable about Lytton, which often is in adventurers; which amounts to a suspicion that there was something in him after all. It rang out of him when he said to the hesitating Crimean Parliament: "Destroy your Government and save your army."

With the next phase of Victorian fiction we enter a new world; the later, more revolutionary, more continental, freer but in some ways weaker world in which we live to-day. The subtle and sad change that was passing like twilight across the English brain at this time is very well expressed in the fact that men have come to mention the great name of Meredith in the same breath as Mr. Thomas Hardy. Both writers, doubtless, disagreed with the orthodox religion of the ordinary English village. Most of us have disagreed with that religion until we made the simple discovery that it does not exist. But in any age where ideas could be even feebly disentangled from each other, it would have been evident at once that Meredith and Hardy were, intellectually speaking, mortal enemies.

They were much more opposed to each other than Newman was to Kingsley; or than Abelard was to St. Bernard. But then they collided in a sceptical age, which is like colliding in a London fog. There can never be any clear controversy in a sceptical age.

Nevertheless both Hardy and Meredith did mean something; and they did mean diametrically opposite things. Meredith was perhaps the only man in the modern world who has almost had the high honour of rising out of the low estate of a Pantheist into the high estate of a Pagan. A Pagan is a person who can do what hardly any person for the last two thousand years could do: a person who can take Nature naturally. It is due to Meredith to say that no one outside a few of the great Greeks has ever taken Nature so naturally as he did. And it is also due to him to say that no one outside Colney Hatch ever took Nature so unnaturally as it was taken in what Mr. Hardy has had the blasphemy to call Wessex Tales. This division between the two points of view is vital; because the turn of the nineteenth century was a very sharp one; by it we have reached the rapids in which we find ourselves to-day.

Meredith really is a Pantheist. You can express it by saying that God is the great All: you can express it much more intelligently by saying that Pan is the great god. But there is some sense in it, and the sense is this: that some people believe that this world is sufficiently good at bottom for us to trust ourselves to it without very much knowing why. It is the whole point in most of Meredith's tales that there is something behind us that often saves us when we understand neither it nor ourselves. He sometimes talked mere intellectualism about women: but that is because the most brilliant brains can get tired. Meredith's brain was quite tired when it wrote some of its most quoted and least interesting epigrams: like that about passing Seraglio Point, but not doubling Cape Turk. Those who can see Meredith's mind in that are with those who can see Dickens' mind in Little Nell. Both were chivalrous pronouncements on behalf of oppressed females: neither has any earthly meaning as ideas.

But what Meredith did do for women was not to emancipate them (which means nothing) but to express them, which means a great deal. And he often expressed them right, even when he expressed himself wrong. Take, for instance, that phrase so often quoted: "Woman will be the last thing civilised by man." Intellectually it is something worse than false; it is the opposite of what he was always attempting to say. So far from admitting any equality in the sexes, it logically admits that a man may use against a woman any chains or whips he has been in the habit of using against a tiger or a bear. He stood as the special champion of female dignity: but I cannot remember any author, Eastern or Western, who has so calmly assumed that man is the master and woman merely the material, as Meredith really does in this phrase. Any one who knows a free woman (she is generally a married woman) will immediately be inclined to ask two simple and catastrophic questions, first: "Why should woman be civilised?" and, second: "Why, if she is to be civilised, should she be civilised by man?" In the mere intellectualism of the matter, Meredith seems to be talking the most brutal sex mastery: he, at any rate, has not doubled Cape Turk, nor even passed

Seraglio Point. Now why is it that we all really feel that this Meredithian passage is not so insolently masculine as in mere logic it would seem? I think it is for this simple reason: that there is something about Meredith making us feel that it is not woman he disbelieves in, but civilisation. It is a dark undemonstrated feeling that Meredith would really be rather sorry if woman were civilised by man—or by anything else. When we have got that, we have got the real Pagan—the man that does believe in Pan.

It is proper to put this philosophic matter first, before the æsthetic appreciation of Meredith, because with Meredith a sort of passing bell has rung and the Victorian orthodoxy is certainly no longer safe. Dickens and Carlyle, as we have said, rebelled against the orthodox compromise: but Meredith has escaped from it. Cosmopolitanism, Socialism, Feminism are already in the air; and Queen Victoria has begun to look like Mrs. Grundy. But to escape from a city is one thing: to choose a road is another. The free-thinker who found himself outside the Victorian city, found himself also in the fork of two very different naturalistic paths. One of them went upwards through a tangled but living forest to lonely but healthy hills: the other went down to a swamp. Hardy went down to botanise in the swamp, while Meredith climbed towards the sun. Meredith became, at his best, a sort of daintily dressed Walt Whitman: Hardy became a sort of village atheist brooding and blaspheming over the village idiot. It is largely because the free-thinkers, as a school, have hardly made up their minds whether they want to be more optimist or more pessimist than Christianity that their small but sincere movement has failed.

For the duel is deadly; and any agnostic who wishes to be anything more than a Nihilist must sympathise with one version of nature or the other. The God of Meredith is impersonal; but he is often more healthy and kindly than any of the persons. That of Thomas Hardy is almost made personal by the intense feeling that he is poisonous. Nature is always coming in to save Meredith's women; Nature is always coming in to betray and ruin Hardy's. It has been said that if God had not existed it would have been necessary to invent Him. But it is not often, as in Mr. Hardy's case, that it is necessary to invent Him in order to prove how unnecessary (and undesirable) He is. But Mr. Hardy is anthropomorphic out of sheer atheism. He personifies the universe in order to give it a piece of his mind. But the fight is unequal for the old philosophical reason: that the universe had already given Mr. Hardy a piece of *its* mind to fight with. One curious result of this divergence in the two types of sceptic is this: that when these two brilliant novelists break down or blow up or otherwise lose for a moment their artistic self-command, they are both equally wild, but wild in opposite directions. Meredith shows an extravagance in comedy which, if it were not so complicated, every one would call broad farce. But Mr. Hardy has the honour of inventing a new sort of game, which may be called the extravagance of depression. The placing of the weak lover and his new love in such a place that they actually see the black flag announcing that Tess has been hanged is utterly inexcusable in art and probability; it is a cruel practical joke. But it is a practical joke at which even its author cannot brighten up enough to laugh.

But it is when we consider the great artistic power of these two writers, with all their eccentricities, that we see even more clearly that free-thought was, as it were, a fight between finger-posts. For it is the remarkable fact that it was the man who had the healthy and manly outlook who had the crabbed and perverse style; it was the man who had the crabbed and perverse outlook who had the healthy and manly style. The reader may well have complained of paradox when I observed above that Meredith, unlike most neo-Pagans, did in his way take Nature naturally. It may be suggested, in tones of some remonstrance, that things like "though pierced by the cruel acerb," or "thy fleetingness is bigger in the ghost," or "her gabbling grey she eyes askant," or "sheer film of the surface awag" are not taking Nature naturally. And this is true of Meredith's style, but it is not true of his spirit; nor even, apparently, of his serious opinions. In one of the poems I have quoted he actually says of those who live nearest to that Nature he was always praising—

"Have they but held her laws and nature dear,
They mouth no sentence of inverted wit";

which certainly was what Meredith himself was doing most of the time. But a similar paradox of the combination of plain tastes with twisted phrases can also be seen in Browning. Something of the same can be seen in many of the cavalier poets. I do not understand it: it may be that the fertility of a cheerful mind crowds everything, so that the tree is entangled in its own branches; or it may be that the cheerful mind cares less whether it is understood or not; as a man is less articulate when he is humming than when he is calling for help.

Certainly Meredith suffers from applying a complex method to men and things he does not mean to be complex; nay, honestly admires for being simple. The conversations between Diana and Redworth fail of their full contrast because Meredith can afford the twopence for Diana coloured, but cannot afford the penny for Redworth plain. Meredith's ideals were neither sceptical nor finicky: but they can be called insufficient. He had, perhaps, over and above his honest Pantheism two convictions profound enough to be called prejudices. He was probably of Welsh blood, certainly of Celtic sympathies, and he set himself more swiftly though more subtly than Ruskin or Swinburne to undermining the enormous complacency of John Bull. He also had a sincere hope in the strength of womanhood, and may be said, almost without hyperbole, to have begotten gigantic daughters. He may yet suffer for his chivalric interference as many champions do. I have little doubt that when St. George had killed the dragon he was heartily afraid of the princess. But certainly neither of these two vital enthusiasms touched the Victorian trouble. The disaster of the modern English is not that they are not Celtic, but that they are not English. The tragedy of the modern woman is not that she is not allowed to follow man, but that she follows him far too slavishly. This conscious and theorising Meredith did not get very near his problem and is certainly miles away from ours. But the other Meredith was a creator; which means a god. That is true of him which is true of so different a man as Dickens, that all one can say of him is that he is full of good things. A reader opening one of his books feels like a schoolboy opening a hamper which he knows to have somehow cost a hundred pounds. He may be more bewildered by it than by an ordinary hamper; but he gets the impression of a real richness of thought; and that is what one really gets from such riots of felicity as *Evan Harrington* or *Harry Richmond*. His philosophy may be barren, but he was not. And the chief feeling among those that enjoy him is a mere wish that more people could enjoy him too.

I end here upon Hardy and Meredith; because this parting of the ways to open optimism and open pessimism really was the end of the Victorian peace. There are many other men, very nearly as great, on whom I might delight to linger: on Shorthouse, for instance, who in one way goes with Mrs. Browning or Coventry Patmore. I mean that he has a wide culture, which is called by some a narrow religion. When we think what even the best novels about cavaliers have been (written by men like Scott or Stevenson) it is a wonderful thing that the author of *John Inglesant* could write a cavalier romance in which he forgot Cromwell but remembered Hobbes. But Shorthouse is outside the period in fiction in the same sort of way in which Francis Thompson is outside it in poetry. He did not accept the Victorian basis. He knew too much.

There is one more matter that may best be considered here, though briefly: it illustrates the extreme difficulty of dealing with the Victorian English in a book like this, because of their eccentricity; not of opinions, but of character and artistic form. There are several great Victorians who will not fit into any of the obvious categories I employ; because they will not fit into anything, hardly into the world itself. Where Germany or Italy would relieve the monotony of mankind by paying serious respect to an artist, or a scholar, or a patriotic warrior, or a priest—it was always the instinct of the English to do it by pointing out a Character. Dr. Johnson has faded as a poet or a critic, but he survives as a Character. Cobbett is neglected (unfortunately) as a publicist and pamphleteer, but he is remembered as a Character. Now these people continued to crop up through the Victorian time; and each stands so much by himself that I shall end these pages with a profound suspicion that I have forgotten to mention a Character of gigantic dimensions. Perhaps the best example of such eccentrics is George Borrow; who sympathised with unsuccessful nomads like the gipsies while every one else sympathised with successful nomads like the Jews; who had a genius like the west wind for the awakening of wild and casual friendships and the drag and attraction of the roads. But whether George Borrow ought to go into the section devoted to philosophers, or the section devoted to novelists, or the section de voted to liars, nobody else has ever known, even if he did.

But the strongest case of this Victorian power of being abruptly original in a corner can be found in two things: the literature meant merely for children and the literature meant merely for fun. It is true that these two very Victorian things often melted into each other (as was the way of Victorian things), but not sufficiently to make it safe to mass them together without distinction. Thus there was George Macdonald, a Scot of genius as genuine as Carlyle's; he could write fairy-tales that made all experience a fairy-tale. He could give the real sense that every one had the end of an elfin thread that must at last lead them into

Paradise. It was a sort of optimist Calvinism. But such really significant fairytales were accidents of genius. Of the Victorian Age as a whole it is true to say that it did discover a new thing; a thing called Nonsense. It may be doubted whether this thing was really invented to please children. Rather it was invented by old people trying to prove their first childhood, and sometimes succeeding only in proving their second. But whatever else the thing was, it was English and it was individual. Lewis Carroll gave mathematics a holiday: he carried logic into the wild lands of illogicality. Edward Lear, a richer, more romantic and therefore more truly Victorian buffoon, improved the experiment. But the more we study it, the more we shall, I think, conclude that it reposed on something more real and profound in the Victorians than even their just and exquisite appreciation of children. It came from the deep Victorian sense of humour.

It may appear, because I have used from time to time the only possible phrases for the case, that I mean the Victorian Englishman to appear as a blockhead, which means an unconscious buffoon. To all this there is a final answer: that he was also a conscious buffoon—and a successful one. He was a humorist; and one of the best humorists in Europe. That which Goethe had never taught the Germans, Byron did manage to teach the English—the duty of not taking him seriously. The strong and shrewd Victorian humour appears in every slash of the pencil of Charles Keene; in every undergraduate inspiration of Calverley or "Q." or J. K. S. They had largely forgotten both art and arms: but the gods had left them laughter.

But the final proof that the Victorians were alive by this laughter, can be found in the fact they could manage and master for a moment even the cosmopolitan modern theatre. They could contrive to put "The Bab Ballads" on the stage. To turn a private name into a public epithet is a thing given to few: but the word "Gilbertian" will probably last longer than the name Gilbert.

It meant a real Victorian talent; that of exploding unexpectedly and almost, as it seemed, unintentionally. Gilbert made good jokes by the thousand; but he never (in his best days) made the joke that could possibly have been expected of him. This is the last essential of the Victorian. Laugh at him as a limited man, a moralist, conventionalist, an opportunist, a formalist. But remember also that he was really a humorist; and may still be laughing at you.

CHAPTER III

THE GREAT VICTORIAN POETS

What was really unsatisfactory in Victorian literature is something much easier to feel than to state. It was not so much a superiority in the men of other ages to the Victorian men. It was a superiority of Victorian men to themselves. The individual was unequal. Perhaps that is why the society became unequal: I cannot say. They were lame giants; the strongest of them walked on one leg a little shorter than the other. A great man in any age must be a common man, and also an uncommon man. Those that are only uncommon men are perverts and sowers of pestilence. But somehow the great Victorian man was more and less than this. He was at once a giant and a dwarf. When he has been sweeping the sky in circles infinitely great, he suddenly shrivels into something indescribably small. There is a moment when Carlyle turns suddenly from a high creative mystic to a common Calvinist. There are moments when George Eliot turns from a prophetess into a governess. There are also moments when Ruskin turns into a governess, without even the excuse of sex. But in all these cases the alteration comes as a thing quite abrupt and unreasonable. We do not feel this acute angle anywhere in Homer or in Virgil or in Chaucer or in Shakespeare or in Dryden; such things as they knew they knew. It is no disgrace to Homer that he had not discovered Britain; or to Virgil that he had not discovered America; or to Chaucer that he had not discovered the solar system; or to Dryden that he had not discovered the steam-engine. But we do most frequently feel, with the Victorians, that the very vastness of the number of things they know illustrates the abrupt abyss of the things they do not know. We feel, in a sort of way, that it *is* a disgrace to a man like Carlyle when he asks the Irish why they do not bestir themselves and re-forest their country: saying not a word about the soaking up of every sort of profit by the landlords which made that and every other Irish improvement impossible. We feel that it *is* a disgrace to a man like Ruskin when he says, with a solemn visage, that building in iron is ugly and unreal, but that the weightiest objection is that there is no mention of it in the Bible; we feel as if he had just said he could find no hair-brushes in Habakkuk. We feel that it *is* a disgrace to a man like Thackeray when he proposes that people should be forcibly prevented from being nuns, merely because he has no fixed intention of becoming a nun himself. We feel that it *is* a disgrace to a man like Tennyson, when he talks of the French revolutions, the huge crusades that had recreated the whole of his civilisation, as being "no graver than a schoolboy's barring out." We feel that it *is* a disgrace to a man like Browning to make spluttering and spiteful puns about the names Newman, Wiseman, and Manning. We feel that it *is* a disgrace to a man like Newman when he confesses that for some time he felt as if he couldn't come in to the Catholic Church, because of that dreadful Mr. Daniel O'Connell, who had the vulgarity to fight for his own country. We feel that it *is* a disgrace to a man like Dickens, when he makes a blind brute and savage out of a man like St. Dunstan; it sounds as if it were not Dickens talking but Dombey. We feel it *is* a disgrace to a man like Swinburne, when he has a Jingo fit and calls the Boer children in the concentration camps "Whelps of treacherous dams whom none save we have spared to starve and slay": we feel that Swinburne, for the first time, really has become an immoral and indecent writer. All this is a certain odd provincialism peculiar to the English in that great century: they were in a kind of pocket; they appealed to too narrow a public opinion; I am certain that no French or German men of the same genius made such remarks. Renan was the enemy of the Catholic Church; but who can imagine Renan writing of it as Kingsley or Dickens did? Taine was the enemy of the French Revolution; but who can imagine Taine talking about it as Tennyson or Newman talked? Even Matthew Arnold, though he saw this peril and prided himself on escaping it, did not altogether escape it. There must be (to use an Irishism) something shallow in the depths of any man who talks about the *Zeitgeist* as if it were a living thing.

But this defect is very specially the key to the case of the two great Victorian poets, Tennyson and Browning; the two spirited or beautiful tunes, so to speak, to which the other events marched or danced. It was especially so of Tennyson, for a reason which raises some of the most real problems about his poetry. Tennyson, of course, owed a great deal to Virgil. There is no question of plagiarism here; a debt to Virgil is like a debt to Nature. But Tennyson was a provincial Virgil. In such passages as that about the schoolboy's barring out he might be called a suburban Virgil. I mean that he tried to have the universal balance of all the ideas at which the great Roman had aimed: but he hadn't got hold of all the ideas to balance. Hence his work was not a balance of truths, like the universe. It was a balance of whims; like the British Constitution. It is intensely typical of Tennyson's philosophical temper that he was almost the only Poet Laureate who was not ludicrous. It is not absurd to think of Tennyson as tuning his harp in praise of Queen Victoria: that is, it is not absurd in the same sense as Chaucer's harp hallowed by dedication to Richard II or Wordsworth's harp hallowed by dedication to George IV is absurd. Richard's court could not properly appreciate either Chaucer's daisies or his "devotion." George IV would not have gone pottering about Helvellyn in search of purity and the simple annals of the poor. But Tennyson did sincerely believe in the Victorian compromise; and sincerity is never undignified. He really did hold a great many of the same views as Queen Victoria, though he was gifted with a more fortunate literary style. If Dickens is Cobbett's democracy stirring in its grave, Tennyson is the exquisitely ornamental extinguisher on the flame of the first revolutionary poets. England has settled down; England has become Victorian. The compromise was interesting, it was national and for a long time it was successful: there is still a great deal to be said for it. But it was as freakish and unphilosophic, as arbitrary and untranslatable, as a beggar's patched coat or a child's secret language. Now it is here that Browning had a certain odd advantage over Tennyson; which has, perhaps, somewhat exaggerated his intellectual superiority to him. Browning's eccentric style was more suitable to the poetry of a nation of eccentrics; of people for the time being removed far from the centre of intellectual interests. The hearty and pleasant task of expressing one's intense dislike of something one doesn't understand is much more poetically achieved by saying, in a general way "Grrr—you swine!" than it is by laboured lines such as "the red fool-fury of the Seine." We all feel that there is more of the man in Browning here; more of Dr. Johnson or Cobbett. Browning is the Englishman taking himself wilfully, following his nose like a bull-dog, going by his own likes and dislikes. We cannot help feeling that Tennyson is the Englishman taking himself seriously—an awful sight. One's memory flutters unhappily over a certain letter about the Papal Guards written by Sir Willoughby Patterne. It is here chiefly that Tennyson suffers by that very Virgilian loveliness and dignity of diction which he put to the service of such a small and anomalous national scheme. Virgil had the best news to tell as well as the best words to tell it in. His world might be sad; but it was the largest world one could live in before the coming of Christianity. If he told the Romans to spare the vanquished and to war down the mighty, at least he was more or less well informed about who *were* mighty and who *were* vanquished. But when Tennyson wrote verses like—

"Of freedom in her regal seat,
Of England; not the schoolboy heat,
The blind hysterics of the Celt"

he quite literally did not know one word of what he was talking about; he did not know what Celts are, or what hysterics are, or what freedom was, or what regal was or even of what England was—in the living Europe of that time.

His religious range was very much wider and wiser than his political; but here also he suffered from treating as true universality a thing that was only a sort of lukewarm local patriotism. Here also he suffered by the very splendour and perfection of his poetical powers. He was quite the opposite of the man who cannot express himself; the inarticulate singer who dies with all his music in him. He had a great deal to say; but he had much more power of expression than was wanted for anything he had to express. He could not think up to the height of his own towering style.

For whatever else Tennyson was, he was a great poet; no mind that feels itself free, that is, above the ebb and flow of fashion, can feel anything but contempt for the later effort to discredit him in that respect. It is true that, like Browning and almost every other Victorian poet, he was really two poets. But it is just to him to insist that in his case (unlike Browning's) both the poets were good. The first is more or less like Stevenson in metre; it is a magical luck or skill in the mere choice of words. "Wet sands marbled with moon and cloud"—"Flits by the sea-blue bird of March"—"Leafless ribs and iron horns"—"When the long dun wolds are ribbed with snow"—in all these cases one word is the keystone of an arch which would fall into ruin without it. But there are other strong phrases that recall not Stevenson but rather their common master, Virgil—"Tears from the depths of some divine despair"—"There is fallen a splendid tear from the passion-flower at the gate"—"Was a great water; and the moon was full"—"God made Himself an awful rose of dawn." These do not depend on a word but on an idea: they might even be translated. It is also true, I think, that he was first and last a lyric poet. He was always best when he expressed himself shortly. In long poems he had an unfortunate habit of eventually saying very nearly the opposite of what he meant to say. I will take only two instances of what I mean. In the *Idylls of the King*, and in *In Memoriam* (his two sustained and ambitious efforts), particular phrases are always flashing out the whole fire of the truth; the truth that Tennyson meant. But owing to his English indolence, his English aristocratic irresponsibility, his English vagueness in thought, he always managed to make the main poem mean exactly what he did not mean. Thus, these two lines which simply say that

"Lancelot was the first in tournament,
But Arthur mightiest in the battle-field"

do really express what he meant to express about Arthur being after all "the highest, yet most human too; not Lancelot, nor another." But as his hero is actually developed, we have exactly the opposite impression; that poor old Lancelot, with all his faults, was much more of a man than Arthur. He was a Victorian in the bad as well as the good sense; he could not keep priggishness out of long poems. Or again, take the case of *In Memoriam*. I will quote one verse (probably incorrectly) which has always seemed to me splendid, and which does express what the whole poem should express—but hardly does.

"That we may lift from out the dust,
A voice as unto him that hears
A cry above the conquered years
Of one that ever works, and trust."

The poem should have been a cry above the conquered years. It might well have been that if the poet could have said sharply at the end of it, as a pure piece of dogma, "I've forgotten every feature of the man's face: I know God holds him alive." But under the influence of the mere leisurely length of the thing, the reader *does* rather receive the impression that the wound has been healed only by time; and that the victor hours *can* boast that this is the man that loved and lost, but all he was is overworn. This is not the truth; and Tennyson did not intend it for the truth. It is simply the result of the lack of something militant, dogmatic and structural in him: whereby he could not be trusted with the trail of a very long literary process without entangling himself like a kitten playing cat's-cradle.

Browning, as above suggested, got on much better with eccentric and secluded England because he treated it as eccentric and secluded; a place where one could do what one liked. To a considerable extent he did do what he liked; arousing not a few complaints; and many doubts and conjectures as to why on earth he liked it. Many comparatively sympathetic persons pondered upon what pleasure it could give any man to write *Sordello* or rhyme "end-knot" to "offend not." Nevertheless he was no anarchist and no mystagogue; and even where he was defective, his defect has commonly been stated wrongly. The two chief charges against him were a contempt for form unworthy of an artist, and a poor pride in obscurity. The obscurity is true, though not, I think, the pride in it; but the truth about this charge rather rises out of the truth about the other. The other charge is not true. Browning cared very much for form; he cared very much for style. You may not happen to like his style; but he did. To say that he had not enough mastery over form to express himself perfectly like Tennyson or Swinburne is like criticising the griffin of a mediæval gargoyle without even knowing that it is a griffin; treating it as an infantile and unsuccessful attempt at a classical angel. A poet indifferent to form ought to mean a poet who did not care what form he used as long as he expressed his thoughts. He might be a rather entertaining sort of poet; telling a smoking-room story in blank verse or writing a hunting-song in the Spenserian stanza; giving a realistic analysis of infanticide in a series of triolets; or proving the truth of Immortality in a long string of limericks. Browning certainly had no such indifference. Almost every poem of Browning, especially the shortest and most successful ones, was moulded or graven in some special style, generally grotesque, but invariably deliberate. In most cases whenever he wrote a new song he wrote a new kind of song. The new lyric is not only of a different metre, but of a different shape. No one, not even Browning, ever wrote a poem in the same style as that horrible one beginning "John, Master of the Temple of God," with its weird choruses and creepy prose directions. No one, not even Browning, ever wrote a poem in the same style as *Pisgah-sights*. No one, not even Browning, ever wrote a poem in the same style as *Time's Revenges*. No one, not even Browning, ever wrote a poem in the same style as *Meeting at Night* and *Parting at Morning*. No one, not even Browning, ever wrote a poem in the same style as *The Flight of the Duchess*, or in the same style as *The Grammarian's Funeral*, or in the same style as *A Star*, or in the same style as that astounding lyric which begins abruptly "Some people hang pictures up." These metres and manners were not accidental; they really do suit the sort of spiritual experiment Browning was making in each case. Browning, then, was not chaotic; he was deliberately grotesque. But there certainly was, over and above this grotesqueness, a perversity and irrationality about the man which led him to play the fool in the middle of his own poems; to leave off carving gargoyles and simply begin throwing stones. His curious complicated puns are an example of this: Hood had used the pun to make a sentence or a sentiment especially pointed and clear. In Browning the word with two meanings seems to mean rather less, if anything, than the word with one. It also applies to his trick of setting himself to cope with impossible rhymes. It may be fun, though it is not poetry, to try rhyming to ranunculus; but even the fun presupposes that you *do* rhyme to it; and I will affirm, and hold under persecution, that "Tommy-make-room-for-your-uncle-us" does not rhyme to it.

The obscurity, to which he must in a large degree plead guilty, was, curiously enough, the result rather of the gay artist in him than the deep thinker. It is patience in the Browning students; in Browning it was only impatience. He wanted to say something comic and energetic and he wanted to say it quick. And, between his artistic skill in the fantastic and his temperamental turn for the abrupt, the idea sometimes flashed past unseen. But it is quite an error to suppose that these are the dark mines containing his treasure. The two or three great and true things he really had to say he generally managed to say quite simply. Thus he really did want to say that God had indeed made man and woman one flesh; that the sex relation was religious in this real sense that even in our sin and despair we take it for granted and expect a sort of virtue in it. The feelings of the bad husband about the good wife, for instance, are about as subtle and entangled as any matter on this earth; and Browning really had something to say about them. But he said it in some of the plainest and most unmistakable words in all literature; as lucid as a flash of lightning. "Pompilia, will you let them murder me?" Or again, he did really want to say that death and such moral terrors were best taken in a military spirit; he could not have said it more simply than: "I was ever a fighter; one fight more, the best and the last." He did really wish to say that human life was unworkable unless immortality were implied in it every other moment; he could not have said it more simply: "leave now to dogs and apes; Man has for ever." The obscurities were not merely superficial, but often covered quite superficial ideas. He was as likely as not to be most unintelligible of all in writing a compliment in a lady's album. I remember in my boyhood (when Browning kept us awake like coffee) a friend reading out the poem about the portrait to which I have already referred, reading it in that rapid dramatic way in which this poet must be read. And I was profoundly puzzled at the passage where it seemed to say that the cousin disparaged the picture, "while John scorns ale." I could not think what this sudden teetotalism on the part of John had to do with the affair, but I forgot to ask at the time and it was only years afterwards that, looking at the book, I found it was "John's corns ail," a very Browningesque way of saying he winced. Most of Browning's obscurity is of that sort—the mistakes are almost as quaint as misprints—and the Browning student, in that sense, is more a proof reader than a disciple. For the rest his real religion was of the most manly, even the most boyish sort. He is called an optimist; but the word suggests a calculated contentment which was not in the least one of his vices. What he really was was a romantic. He offered the cosmos as an adventure rather than a scheme. He did not explain evil, far less explain it away; he enjoyed defying it. He was a troubadour even in theology and metaphysics: like the *Jongleurs de Dieu* of St. Francis. He may be said to have serenaded heaven with a guitar, and even, so to speak, tried to climb there with a rope ladder. Thus his most vivid things are the red-hot little love lyrics, or rather, little love dramas. He did one really original and admirable thing: he managed the real details of modern love affairs in verse, and love is the most realistic thing in the world. He substituted the street with the green blind for the faded garden of Watteau, and the "blue spirt of a lighted match" for the monotony of the evening star.

Before leaving him it should be added that he was fitted to deepen the Victorian mind, but not to broaden it. With all his Italian sympathies and Italian residence, he was not the man to get Victorian England out of its provincial rut: on many things Kingsley himself was not so narrow. His celebrated wife was wider and wiser than he in this sense; for she was, however one-sidedly, involved in the emotions of central European politics. She defended Louis Napoleon and Victor Emmanuel; and intelligently, as one conscious of the case against them both. As to why it now seems simple to defend the first Italian King, but absurd to defend the last French Emperor—well, the reason is sad and simple. It is concerned with certain curious things called success and failure, and I ought to have considered it under the heading of *The Book of Snobs*. But Elizabeth Barrett, at least, was no snob: her political poems have rather an impatient air, as if they were written, and even published, rather prematurely—just before the fall of her idol. These old political poems of hers are too little read to-day; they are amongst the most sincere documents on the history of the times, and many modern blunders could be corrected by the reading of them. And Elizabeth Barrett had a strength really rare among women poets; the strength of the phrase. She excelled in her sex, in epigram, almost as much as Voltaire in his. Pointed phrases like: "Martyrs by the pang without the palm"—or "Incense to sweeten a crime and myrrh to embitter a curse," these expressions, which are witty after the old fashion of the conceit, came quite freshly and spontaneously to her quite modern mind. But the first fact is this, that these epigrams of hers were never so true as when they turned on one of the two or three pivots on which contemporary Europe was really turning. She is by far the most European of all the English poets of that age; all of them, even her own much greater husband, look local beside her. Tennyson and the rest are nowhere. Take any positive political fact, such as the final fall of Napoleon. Tennyson wrote these profoundly foolish lines—

"He thought to quell the stubborn hearts of oak
Madman!"

as if the defeat of an English regiment were a violation of the laws of Nature. Mrs. Browning knew no more facts about Napoleon, perhaps, than Tennyson did; but she knew the truth. Her epigram on Napoleon's fall is in one line

"And kings crept out again to feel the sun."

Talleyrand would have clapped his horrible old hands at that. Her instinct about the statesman and the soldier was very like Jane Austen's instinct for the gentleman and the man. It is not unnoticeable that as Miss Austen spent most of her life in a village, Miss Barrett spent most of her life on a sofa. The godlike power of guessing seems (for some reason I do not understand) to grow under such conditions. Unfortunately Mrs. Browning was like all the other Victorians in going a little lame, as I have roughly called it, having one leg shorter than the other. But her case was, in one sense, extreme. She exaggerated both ways. She was too strong and too weak, or (as a false sex philosophy would express it) too masculine and too feminine. I mean that she hit the centre of weakness with almost the same emphatic precision with which she hit the centre of strength. She could write finally of the factory wheels "grinding life down from its mark," a strong and strictly true observation. Unfortunately she could also write of Euripides "with his droppings of warm tears." She could write in *A Drama of Exile*, a really fine exposition, touching the later relation of Adam and the animals: unfortunately the tears were again turned on at the wrong moment at the main; and the stage direction commands a silence, only broken by the dropping of angel's tears. How much noise is made by angel's tears? Is it a sound of emptied buckets, or of garden hose, or of mountain cataracts? That is the sort of question which Elizabeth Barrett's extreme love of the extreme was always tempting people to ask. Yet the question, as asked, does her a heavy historical injustice; we remember all the lines in her work which were weak enough to be called "womanly," we forget the multitude of strong lines that are strong enough to be called "manly"; lines that Kingsley or Henley would have jumped for joy to print in proof of their manliness. She had one of the peculiar talents of true rhetoric, that of a powerful concentration. As to the critic who thinks her poetry owed anything to the great poet who was her husband, he can go and live in the same hotel with the man who can believe that George Eliot owed anything to the extravagant imagination of Mr. George Henry Lewes. So far from Browning inspiring or interfering, he did not in one sense interfere enough. Her real inferiority to him in literature is that he was consciously while she was unconsciously absurd.

It is natural, in the matter of Victorian moral change, to take Swinburne as the next name here. He is the only poet who was also, in the European sense, on the spot; even if, in the sense of the Gilbertian song, the spot was barred. He also knew that something rather crucial was happening to Christendom; he thought it was getting unchristened. It is even a little amusing, indeed, that these two Pro-Italian poets almost conducted a political correspondence in rhyme. Mrs. Browning sternly reproached those who had ever doubted the good faith of the King of Sardinia, whom she acclaimed as being truly a king. Swinburne, lyrically alluding to her as "Sea-eagle of English feather," broadly hinted that the chief blunder of that wild fowl had been her support of an autocratic adventurer: "calling a crowned man royal, that was no more than a king." But it is not fair, even in this important connection, to judge Swinburne by *Songs Before Sunrise*. They were songs before a sunrise that has never turned up. Their dogmatic assertions have for a long time past stared starkly at us as nonsense. As, for instance, the phrase "Glory to Man in the Highest, for man is the master of things"; after which there is evidently nothing to be said, except that it is not true. But even where Swinburne had his greater grip, as in that grave and partly just poem *Before a Crucifix*, Swinburne, the most Latin, the most learned, the most largely travelled of the Victorians, still knows far less of the facts than even Mrs. Browning. The whole of the poem, *Before a Crucifix*, breaks down by one mere mistake. It imagines that the French or Italian peasants who fell on their knees before the Crucifix did so because they were slaves. They fell on their knees because they were free men, probably owning their own farms. Swinburne could have found round about Putney plenty of slaves who had no crucifixes: but only crucifixions.

When we come to ethics and philosophy, doubtless we find Swinburne in full revolt, not only against the temperate idealism of Tennyson, but against the genuine piety and moral enthusiasm of people like Mrs. Browning. But here again Swinburne is very English, nay, he is very Victorian, for his revolt is illogical. For the purposes of intelligent insurrection against priests and kings, Swinburne ought to have described the natural life of man, free and beautiful, and proved from this both the noxiousness and the needlessness of such chains. Unfortunately Swinburne rebelled against Nature first and then tried to rebel against religion for doing exactly the same thing that he had done. His songs of joy are not really immoral; but his songs of sorrow are. But when he merely hurls at the priest the assertion that flesh is grass and life is sorrow, he really lays himself open to the restrained answer, "So I have ventured, on various occasions, to remark." When he went forth, as it were, as the champion of pagan change and pleasure, he heard uplifted the grand choruses of his own *Atalanta*, in his rear, refusing hope.

The splendid diction that blazes through the whole of that drama, that still dances exquisitely in the more lyrical *Poems and Ballads*, makes some marvellous appear ances in *Songs Before Sunrise*, and then mainly falters and fades away, is, of course, the chief thing about Swinburne. The style is the man; and some will add that it does not, thus unsupported, amount to much of a man. But the style itself suffers some injustice from those who would speak thus. The views expressed are often quite foolish and often quite insincere; but the style itself is a manlier and more natural thing than is commonly made out. It is not in the least languorous or luxurious or merely musical and sensuous, as one would gather from both the eulogies and the satires, from the conscious and the unconscious imitations. On the contrary, it is a sort of fighting and profane parody of the Old Testament; and its lines are made of short English words like the short Roman swords. The first line of one of his finest poems, for instance, runs, "I have lived long enough to have seen one thing, that love hath an end." In that sentence only one small "e" gets outside the monosyllable. Through all his interminable tragedies, he was fondest of lines like—

"If ever I leave off to honour you
God give me shame; I were the worst churl born."

The dramas were far from being short and dramatic; but the words really were. Nor was his verse merely smooth; except his very bad verse, like "the lilies and languors of virtue, to the raptures and roses of vice," which both, in cheapness of form and foolishness of sentiment, may be called the worst couplet in the world's literature. In his real poetry (even in the same poem) his rhythm and rhyme are as original and ambitious as Browning; and the only difference between him and Browning is, not that he is smooth and without ridges, but that he always crests the ridge triumphantly and Browning often does not—

"On thy bosom though many a kiss be,
There are none such as knew it of old.
Was it Alciphron once or Arisbe,
Male ringlets or feminine gold,
That thy lips met with under the statue
Whence a look shot out sharp after thieves
From the eyes of the garden-god at you
Across the fig-leaves."

Look at the rhymes in that verse, and you will see they are as stiff a task as Browning's: only they are successful. That is the real strength of Swinburne—a style. It was a style that nobody could really imitate; and least of all Swinburne himself, though he made the attempt all through his later years. He was, if ever there was one, an inspired poet. I do not think it the highest sort of poet. And you never discover who is an inspired poet until the inspiration goes.

With Swinburne we step into the circle of that later Victorian influence which was very vaguely called Æsthetic. Like all human things, but especially Victorian things, it was not only complex but confused. Things in it that were at one on the emotional side were flatly at war on the intellectual. In the section of the painters, it was the allies or pupils of Ruskin, pious, almost painfully exact, and copying mediæval details rather for their truth than their beauty. In the section of the poets it was pretty loose, Swinburne being the leader of the revels. But there was one great man who was in both sections, a painter and a poet, who may be said to bestride the chasm like a giant. It is in an odd and literal sense true that the name of Rossetti is important here, for the name implies the nationality. I have loosely called Carlyle and the Brontës the romance from the North; the nearest to a general definition of the Æsthetic movement is to call it the romance from the South. It is that warm wind that had never blown so strong since Chaucer, standing in his cold English April, had smelt the spring in Provence. The Englishman has always found it easier to get inspiration from the Italians than from the French; they call to each other across that unconquered castle of reason. Browning's *Englishman in Italy*, Browning's *Italian in England*, were both happier than either would have been in France. Rossetti was the Italian in England, as Browning was the Englishman in Italy; and the first broad fact about the artistic revolution Rossetti wrought is written when we have written his name. But if the South lets in warmth or heat, it also lets in hardness. The more the orange tree is luxuriant in growth, the less it is loose in outline. And it is exactly where the sea is slightly warmer than marble that it looks slightly harder. This, I think, is the one universal power behind the Æsthetic and Pre-Raphaelite movements, which all agreed in two things at least: strictness in the line and strength, nay violence, in the colour.

Rossetti was a remarkable man in more ways than one; he did not succeed in any art; if he had he would probably never have been heard of. It was his happy knack of half failing in both the arts that has made him a success. If he had been as good a poet as Tennyson, he would have been a poet who painted pictures. If he had been as good a painter as Burne-Jones, he would have been a painter who wrote poems. It is odd to note on the very threshold of the extreme art movement that this great artist largely succeeded by not defining his art. His poems were too pictorial. His pictures were too poetical. That is why they really conquered the cold satisfaction of the Victorians, because they did mean something, even if it was a small artistic thing.

Rossetti was one with Ruskin, on the one hand, and Swinburne on the other, in reviving the decorative instinct of the Middle Ages. While Ruskin, in letters only, praised that decoration Rossetti and his friends repeated it. They almost made patterns of their poems. That frequent return of the refrain which was foolishly discussed by Professor Nordau was, in Rossetti's case, of such sadness as sometimes to amount to sameness. The criticism on him, from a mediæval point of view, is not that he insisted on a chorus, but that he could not insist on a jolly chorus. Many of his poems were truly mediæval, but they would have been even more mediæval if he could ever have written such a refrain as "Tally Ho!" or even "Tooral-ooral" instead of "Tall Troy's on fire." With Rossetti goes, of course, his sister, a real poet, though she also illustrated that Pre-Raphaelite's conflict of views that covered their coincidence of taste. Both used the angular outlines, the burning transparencies, the fixed but still unfathomable symbols of the great mediæval civilisation; but Rossetti used the religious imagery (on the whole) irreligiously, Christina Rossetti used it religiously but (on the whole) so to make it seem a narrower religion.

One poet, or, to speak more strictly, one poem, belongs to the same general atmosphere and impulse as Swinburne; the free but languid atmosphere of later Victorian art. But this time the wind blew from hotter and heavier gardens than the gardens of Italy. Edward Fitzgerald, a cultured eccentric, a friend of Tennyson, produced what professed to be a translation of the Persian poet Omar, who wrote quatrains about wine and roses and things in general. Whether the Persian original, in its own Persian way, was greater or less than this version I must not discuss here, and could not discuss anywhere. But it is quite clear that Fitzgerald's work is much too good to be a good translation. It is as personal and creative a thing as ever was written; and the best expression of a bad mood, a mood that may, for all I know, be permanent in Persia, but was certainly at this time particularly fashionable in England. In the technical sense of literature it is one of the most remarkable achievements of that age; as poetical as Swinburne and far more perfect. In this verbal sense its most arresting quality is a combination of something haunting and harmonious that flows by like a river or a song, with something else that is compact and pregnant like a pithy saying picked out in rock by the chisel of some pagan philosopher. It is at once a tune that escapes and an inscription that remains. Thus, alone among the reckless and romantic verses that first rose in Coleridge or Keats, it preserves something also of the wit and civilisation of the eighteenth century. Lines like "a Muezzin from the tower of darkness cries," or "Their mouths are stopped with dust" are successful in the same sense as "Pinnacled dim in the intense inane" or "Through verdurous glooms and winding mossy ways." But—

"Indeed, indeed, repentance oft before
I swore; but was I sober when I swore?"

is equally successful in the same sense as—

"Damn with faint praise, assent with civil leer
And without sneering teach the rest to sneer."

It thus earned a right to be considered the complete expression of that scepticism and sensual sadness into which later Victorian literature was more and more falling away: a sort of bible of unbelief. For a cold fit had followed the hot fit of Swinburne, which was of a feverish sort: he had set out to break down without having, or even thinking he had, the rudiments of rebuilding in him; and he effected nothing national even in the way of destruction. The Tennysonians still walked past him as primly as a young ladies' school—the Browningites still inked their eyebrows and minds in looking for the lost syntax of Browning; while Browning himself was away looking for God, rather in the spirit of a truant boy from their school looking for birds' nests. The nineteenth-century sceptics did not really shake the respectable world and alter it, as the eighteenth-century sceptics had done; but that was because the eighteenth-century sceptics were something more than sceptics, and believed in Greek tragedies, in Roman laws, in the Republic. The Swinburnian sceptics had nothing to fight for but a frame of mind; and when ordinary English people listened to it, they came to the conclusion that it was a frame of mind they would rather hear about than experience. But these later poets did, so to speak, spread their soul in all the empty spaces; weaker brethren, disappointed artists, unattached individuals, very young people, were sapped or swept away by these songs; which, so far as any particular sense in them goes, were almost songs without words. It is because there is something which is after all indescribably manly, intellectual, firm about Fitzgerald's way of phrasing the pessimism that he towers above the slope that was tumbling down to the decadents. But it is still pessimism, a thing unfit for a white man; a thing like opium, that may often be a poison and sometimes a medicine, but never a food for us, who are driven by an inner command not only to think but to live, not only to live but to grow, and not only to grow but to build.

And, indeed, we see the insufficiency of such sad extremes even in the next name among the major poets; we see the Swinburnian parody of mediævalism, the inverted Catholicism of the decadents, struggling to get back somehow on its feet. The æsthetic school had, not quite unjustly, the name of mere dilettanti. But it is fair to say that in the next of them, a workman and a tradesman, we already feel something of that return to real issues leading up to the real revolts that broke up Victorianism at last. In the mere art of words, indeed, William Morris carried much further than Swinburne or Rossetti the mere imitation of stiff mediæval ornament. The other mediævalists had their modern moments; which were (if they had only known it) much more mediæval than their mediæval moments. Swinburne could write—

"We shall see Buonaparte the bastard
Kick heels with his throat in a rope."

One has an uneasy feeling that William Morris would have written something like —

"And the kin of the ill king Bonaparte
Hath a high gallows for all his part."

Rossetti could, for once in a way, write poetry about a real woman and call her "Jenny." One has a disturbed suspicion that Morris would have called her "Jehanne."

But all that seems at first more archaic and decorative about Morris really arose from the fact that he was more virile and real than either Swinburne or Rossetti. It arose from the fact that he really was, what he so often called himself, a craftsman. He had enough masculine strength to be tidy: that is, after the masculine manner, tidy about his own trade. If his poems were too like wallpapers, it was because he really could make wall papers. He knew that lines of poetry ought to be in a row, as palings ought to be in a row; and he knew that neither palings nor poetry looks any the worse for being simple or even severe. In a sense Morris was all the more creative because he felt the hard limits of creation as he would have felt them if he were not working in words but in wood;

and if he was unduly dominated by the mere conventions of the mediævals, it was largely because they were (whatever else they were) the very finest fraternity of free workmen the world is ever likely to see.

The very things that were urged against Morris are in this sense part of his ethical importance; part of the more promising and wholesome turn he was half unconsciously giving to the movement of modern art. His hazier fellow-Socialists blamed him because he made money; but this was at least in some degree because he made other things to make money: it was part of the real and refreshing fact that at last an æsthete had appeared who could make something. If he was a capitalist, at least he was what later capitalists cannot or will not be —something higher than a capitalist, a tradesman. As compared with aristocrats like Swinburne or aliens like Rossetti, he was vitally English and vitally Victorian. He inherits some of that paradoxical glory which Napoleon gave reluctantly to a nation of shopkeepers. He was the last of that nation; he did not go out golfing: like that founder of the artistic shopman, Samuel Richardson, "he kept his shop, and his shop kept him." The importance of his Socialism can easily be exaggerated. Among other lesser points, he was not a Socialist; he was a sort of Dickensian anarchist. His instinct for titles was always exquisite. It is part of his instinct of decoration: for on a page the title always looks important and the printed mass of matter a mere dado under it. And no one had ever nobler titles than *The Roots of the Mountains* or *The Wood at the End of the World*. The reader feels he hardly need read the fairy-tale because the title is so suggestive. But, when all is said, he never chose a better title than that of his social Utopia, *News from Nowhere*. He wrote it while the last Victorians were already embarked on their bold task of fixing the future—of narrating to-day what has happened to-morrow. They named their books by cold titles suggesting straight corridors of marble—titles like *Looking Backward*. But Morris was an artist as well as an anarchist. *News from Nowhere* is an irresponsible title; and it is an irresponsible book. It does not describe the problem solved; it does not describe wealth either wielded by the State or divided equally among the citizens. It simply describes an undiscovered country where every one feels good-natured all day. That he could even dream so is his true dignity as a poet. He was the first of the Æsthetes to smell mediævalism as a smell of the morning; and not as a mere scent of decay.

With him the poetry that had been peculiarly Victorian practically ends; and, on the whole, it is a happy ending. There are many other minor names of major importance; but for one reason or other they do not derive from the schools that had dominated this epoch as such. Thus Thompson, the author of *The City of Dreadful Night*, was a fine poet; but his pessimism combined with a close pugnacity does not follow any of the large but loose lines of the Swinburnian age. But he was a great person—he knew how to be democratic in the dark. Thus Coventry Patmore was a much greater person. He was bursting with ideas, like Browning—and truer ideas as a rule. He was as eccentric and florid and Elizabethan as Browning; and often in moods and metres that even Browning was never wild enough to think of. No one will ever forget the first time he read

Patmore's hint that the cosmos is a thing that God made huge only "to make dirt cheap"; just as nobody will ever forget the sudden shout he uttered when he first heard Mrs. Todgers asked for the rough outline of a wooden leg. These things are not jokes, but discoveries. But the very fact that Patmore was, as it were, the Catholic Browning, keeps him out of the Victorian atmosphere as such. The Victorian English simply thought him an indecent sentimentalist, as they did all the hot and humble religious diarists of Italy or Spain. Something of the same fate followed the most powerful of that last Victorian group who were called "Minor Poets." They numbered many other fine artists: notably Mr. William Watson, who is truly Victorian in that he made a manly attempt to tread down the decadents and return to the right reason of Wordsworth—

"I have not paid the world
The evil and the insolent courtesy
Of offering it my baseness as a gift."

But none of them were able even to understand Francis Thompson; his sky-scraping humility, his mountains of mystical detail, his occasional and unashamed weakness, his sudden and sacred blasphemies. Perhaps the shortest definition of the Victorian Age is that he stood outside it.

CHAPTER IV

THE BREAK-UP OF THE COMPROMISE

If it be curiously and carefully considered it will, I think, appear more and more true that the struggle between the old spiritual theory and the new material theory in England ended simply in a deadlock; and a deadlock that has endured. It is still impossible to say absolutely that England is a Christian country or a heathen country; almost exactly as it was impossible when Herbert Spencer began to write. Separate elements of both sorts are alive, and even increasingly alive. But neither the believer nor the unbeliever has the impudence to call himself the Englishman. Certainly the great Victorian rationalism has succeeded in doing a damage to religion. It has done what is perhaps the worst of all damages to religion. It has driven it entirely into the power of the religious people. Men like Newman, men like Coventry Patmore, men who would have been mystics in any case, were driven back upon being much more extravagantly religious than they would have been in a religious country. Men like Huxley, men like Kingsley, men like most Victorian men, were equally driven back on being irreligious; that is, on doubting things which men's normal imagination does not necessarily doubt. But certainly the most final and forcible fact is that this war ended like the battle of Sheriffmuir, as the poet says; they both did fight, and both did beat, and both did run away. They have left to their descendants a treaty that has become a dull torture. Men may believe in immortality, and none of the men know why. Men may not believe in miracles, and none of the men know why.

The Christian Church had been just strong enough to check the conquest of her chief citadels. The rationalist movement had been just strong enough to conquer some of her outposts, as it seemed, for ever. Neither was strong enough to expel the other; and Victorian England was in a state which some call liberty and some call lockjaw.

But the situation can be stated another way. There came a time, roughly somewhere about 1880, when the two great positive enthusiasms of Western Europe had for the time exhausted each other—Christianity and the French Revolution. About that time there used to be a sad and not unsympathetic jest going about to the effect that Queen Victoria might very well live longer than the Prince of Wales. Somewhat in the same way, though the republican impulse was hardly a hundred years old and the religious impulse nearly two thousand, yet as far as England was concerned, the old wave and the new seemed to be spent at the same time. On the one hand Darwin, especially through the strong journalistic genius of Huxley, had won a very wide spread though an exceedingly vague victory. I do not mean that Darwin's own doctrine was vague; his was merely one particular hypothesis about how animal variety might have arisen; and that particular hypothesis, though it will always be interesting, is now very much the reverse of secure. But it is only in the strictly scientific world and among strictly scientific men that Darwin's detailed suggestion has largely broken down. The general public impression that he had entirely proved his case (whatever it was) was early arrived at, and still remains. It was and is hazily associated with the negation of religion. But (and this is the important point) it was also associated with the negation of democracy. The same Mid-Victorian muddle-headedness that made people think that "evolution" meant that we need not admit the supremacy of God, also made them think that "survival" meant that we must admit the supremacy of men. Huxley had no hand in spreading these fallacies; he was a fair fighter; and he told his own followers, who spoke thus, most emphatically not to play the fool. He said most strongly that his or any theory of evolution left the old philosophical arguments for a creator, right or wrong, exactly where they were before. He also said most emphatically that any one who used the argument of Nature against the ideal of justice or an equal law, was as senseless as a gardener who should fight on the side of the ill weeds merely because they grew apace. I wish, indeed, that in such a rude summary as this, I had space to do justice to Huxley as a literary man and a moralist. He had a live taste and talent for the English tongue, which he devoted to the task of keeping Victorian rationalism rational. He did not succeed. As so often happens when a rather unhealthy doubt is in the atmosphere, the strongest words of their great captain could not keep the growing crowds of agnostics back from the most hopeless and inhuman extremes of destructive thought. Nonsense not yet quite dead about the folly of allowing the unfit to survive began to be more and more wildly whispered. Such helpless specimens of "advanced thought" are, of course, quite as inconsistent with Darwinism as they are with democracy or with any other intelligent proposition ever offered. But these unintelligent propositions were offered; and the ultimate result was this rather important one: that the harshness of Utilitarianism began to turn into downright tyranny. That beautiful faith in human nature and in freedom which had made delicate the dry air of John Stuart Mill; that robust, romantic sense of justice which had redeemed even the injustices of Macaulay—all that seemed slowly and sadly to be drying up. Under the shock of Darwinism all that was good in the Victorian rationalism shook and dissolved like dust. All that was bad in it abode and clung like clay. The magnificent emancipation evaporated; the mean calculation remained. One could still calculate in clear statistical tables, how many men lived, how many men died. One must not ask how they lived; for that is politics. One must not ask how they died; for that is religion. And religion and politics were ruled out of all the Later Victorian debating clubs; even including the debating club at Westminster. What third thing they were discussing, which was neither religion nor politics, I do not know. I have tried the experiment of reading solidly through a vast number of their records and reviews and discussions; and still I do not know. The only third thing I can think of to balance religion and politics is art; and no one well acquainted with the debates at St. Stephen's will imagine that the art of extreme eloquence was the cause of the confusion. None will maintain that our political masters are removed from us by an infinite artistic superiority in the choice of words. The politicians know nothing of politics, which is their own affair: they know nothing of religion, which is certainly not their affair: it may legitimately be said that they have to do with nothing; they have reached that low and last level where a man knows as little about his own claim, as he does about his enemies'. In any case there can be no doubt about the effect of this particular situation on the problem of ethics and science. The duty of dragging truth out by the tail or the hind leg or any other corner one can possibly get hold of, a perfectly sound duty in itself, had somehow come into collision with the older and larger duty of knowing something about the organism and ends of a creature; or, in the everyday phrase, being able to make head or tail of it. This paradox pursued and tormented the Victorians. They could not or would not see that humanity repels or welcomes the railway-train, simply according to what people come by it. They could not see that one welcomes or smashes the telephone, according to what words one hears in it. They really seem to have felt that the train could be a substitute for its own passengers; or the telephone a substitute for its own voice.

In any case it is clear that a change had begun to pass over scientific inquiry, of which we have seen the culmination in our own day. There had begun that easy automatic habit, of science as an oiled and smooth-running machine, that habit of treating things as obviously unquestionable, when, indeed, they are obviously questionable. This began with vaccination in the Early Victorian Age; it extended to the early licence of vivisection in its later age; it has found a sort of fitting foolscap, or crown of crime and folly, in the thing called Eugenics. In all three cases the point was not so much that the pioneers had not proved their case; it was rather that, by an unexpressed rule of respectability, they were not required to prove it. This rather abrupt twist of the rationalistic mind in the direction of arbitrary power, certainly weakened the Liberal movement from within. And meanwhile it was being weakened by heavy blows from without.

There is a week that is the turn of the year; there was a year that was the turn of the century. About 1870 the force of the French Revolution faltered and fell: the year that was everywhere the death of Liberal ideas: the year when Paris fell: the year when Dickens died. While the new foes of freedom, the sceptics and scientists, were damaging democracy in ideas, the old foes of freedom, the emperors and the kings, were damaging her more heavily in arms. For a moment it almost seemed that the old Tory ring of iron, the Holy Alliance, had recombined against France. But there was just this difference: that the Holy Alliance was now not arguably, but almost avowedly, an Unholy Alliance. It was an alliance between those who still thought they could deny the dignity of man and those who had recently begun to have a bright hope of denying even the dignity of God. Eighteenth-century Prussia was Protestant and probably religious. Nineteenth-century Prussia was almost utterly atheist. Thus the old spirit of liberty felt itself shut up at both ends, that which was called progressive and that which was called reactionary: barricaded by Bismarck with blood and iron and by Darwin by blood and bones. The enormous depression which infects many excellent people born about this time, probably has this cause.

It was a great calamity that the freedom of Wilkes and the faith of Dr. Johnson fought each other. But it was an even worse calamity that they practically killed each other. They killed each other almost simultaneously, like Herminius and Mamilius. Liberalism (in Newman's sense) really did strike Christianity through headpiece and through head; that is, it did daze and stun the ignorant and ill-prepared intellect of the English Christian. And Christianity did smite Liberalism through breastplate and through breast; that is, it did succeed, through arms and all sorts of awful accidents, in piercing more or less to the heart of the Utilitarian —and finding that he had none. Victorian Protestantism had not head enough for the business; Victorian Radicalism had not heart enough for the business. Down fell they dead together, exactly as Macaulay's Lay says, and still stood all who saw them fall almost until the hour at which I write.

This coincident collapse of both religious and political idealism produced a curious cold air of emptiness and real subconscious agnosticism such as is extremely unusual in the history of mankind. It is what Mr. Wells, with his usual verbal delicacy and accuracy, spoke of as that ironical silence that follows a great controversy. It is what people less intelligent than Mr. Wells meant by calling themselves *fin de siècle*; though, of course, rationally speaking, there is no more reason for being sad towards the end of a hundred years than towards the end of five hundred fortnights. There was no arithmetical autumn, but there was a spiritual one. And it came from the fact suggested in the para graphs above; the sense that man's two great inspirations had failed him together. The Christian religion was much more dead in the eighteenth century than it was in the nineteenth century. But the republican enthusiasm was also much more alive. If their scepticism was cold, and their faith even colder, their practical politics were wildly idealistic; and if they doubted the kingdom of heaven, they were gloriously credulous about the chances of it coming on earth. In the same way the old pagan republican feeling was much more dead in the feudal darkness of the eleventh or twelfth centuries, than it was even a century later; but if creative politics were at their lowest, creative theology was almost at its highest point of energy.

The modern world, in fact, had fallen between two stools. It had fallen between that austere old three-legged stool which was the tripod of the cold priestess of Apollo; and that other mystical and mediæval stool that may well be called the Stool of Repentance. It kept neither of the two values as intensely valuable. It could not believe in the bonds that bound men; but, then, neither could it believe in the men they bound. It was always restrained in its hatred of slavery by a half remembrance of its yet greater hatred of liberty. They were almost alone, I think, in thus carrying to its extreme the negative attitude already noted in Miss Arabella Allen. Anselm would have despised a civic crown, but he would not have despised a relic. Voltaire would have despised a relic; but he would not have despised a vote. We hardly find them both despised till we come to the age of Oscar Wilde.

These years that followed on that double disillusionment were like one long afternoon in a rich house on a rainy day. It was not merely that everybody believed that nothing would happen; it was also that everybody believed that anything happening was even duller than nothing happening. It was in this stale atmosphere that a few flickers of the old Swinburnian flame survived; and were called Art. The great men of the older artistic movement did not live in this time; rather they lived through it. But this time did produce an interregnum of art that had a truth of its own; though that truth was near to being only a consistent lie.

The movement of those called Æsthetes (as satirised in *Patience*) and the movement of those afterwards called Decadents (satirised in Mr. Street's delightful *Autobiography of a Boy*) had the same captain; or at any rate the same bandmaster. Oscar Wilde walked in front of the first procession wearing a sunflower, and in front of the second procession wearing a green carnation. With the æsthetic movement and its more serious elements, I deal elsewhere; but the second appearance of Wilde is also connected with real intellectual influences, largely negative, indeed, but subtle and influential. The mark in most of the arts of this time was a certain quality which those who like it would call "uniqueness of aspect," and those who do not like it "not quite coming off." I mean the thing meant something from one standpoint; but its mark was that the *smallest* change of standpoint made it unmeaning and unthinkable—a foolish joke. A beggar painted by Rembrandt is as solid as a statue, however roughly he is sketched in; the soul can walk all round him like a public monument. We see he would have other aspects; and that they would all be the aspects of a beggar. Even if one did not admit the extraordinary qualities in the painting, one would have to admit the ordinary qualities in the sitter. If it is not a masterpiece it is a man. But a nocturne by Whistler of mist on the Thames is either a masterpiece or it is nothing; it is either a nocturne or a nightmare of childish nonsense. Made in a certain mood, viewed through a certain temperament, conceived under certain conventions, it may be, it often is, an unreplaceable poem, a vision that may never be seen again. But the moment it ceases to be a splendid picture it ceases to be a picture at all. Or, again, if *Hamlet* is not a great tragedy it is an uncommonly good tale. The people and the posture of affairs would still be there even if one thought that Shakespeare's moral attitude was wrong. Just as one could imagine all the other sides of Rembrandt's beggar, so, with the mind's eye (Horatio), one can see all four sides of the castle of Elsinore. One might tell the tale from the point of view of Laërtes or Claudius or Polonius or the gravedigger; and it would still be a good tale and the same tale. But if we take a play like *Pelléas and Mélisande*, we shall find that unless we grasp the particular fairy thread of thought the poet rather hazily flings to us, we cannot grasp anything whatever. Except from one extreme poetic point of view, the thing is not a play; it is not a bad play, it is a mass of clotted nonsense. One whole act describes the lovers going to look for a ring in a distant cave when they both know they have dropped it down a well. Seen from some secret window on some special side of the soul's turret, this might convey a sense of faerie futility in our human life. But it is quite obvious that unless it called forth that one kind of sympathy, it would call forth nothing but laughter and rotten eggs. In the same play the husband chases his wife with a drawn sword, the wife remarking at intervals "I am not gay." Now there may really be an idea in this; the idea of human misfortune coming most cruelly upon the optimism of innocence; that the lonely human heart says, like a child at a party, "I am not enjoying myself as I thought I should." But it is plain that unless one thinks of this idea (and of this idea only) the expression is not in the least unsuccessful pathos; it is very broad and highly successful farce. Maeterlinck and the decadents, in short, may fairly boast of being subtle; but they must not mind if they are called narrow.

This is the spirit of Wilde's work and of most of the literary work done in that time and fashion. It is, as Mr. Arthur Symons said, an attitude; but it is an attitude in the flat, not in the round; not a statue, but the cardboard king in a toy-theatre, which can only be looked at from the front. In Wilde's own poetry we have particularly a perpetually toppling possibility of the absurd; a sense of just falling too short or just going too far. "Plant lilies at my head" has something wrong about it; something silly that is not there in—

"And put a grey stone at my head"

in the old ballad. But even where Wilde was right, he had a way of being right with this excessive strain on the reader's sympathy (and gravity) which was the mark of all these men with a "point of view." There is a very sound sonnet of his in which he begins by lamenting mere anarchy, as hostile to the art and civilisation that were his only gods; but ends by saying—

"And yet
These Christs that die upon the barricades
God knows that I am with them—in some ways."

Now that is really very true; that is the way a man of wide reading and worldly experience, but not ungenerous impulses, does feel about the mere fanatic, who is at once a nuisance to humanity and an honour to human nature. Yet who can read that last line without feeling that Wilde is poised on the edge of a precipice of bathos; that the phrase comes very near to being quite startlingly silly. It is as in the case of Maeterlinck, let the reader move his standpoint one inch nearer the popular standpoint, and there is nothing for the thing but harsh, hostile, unconquerable mirth. Somehow the image of Wilde lolling like an elegant leviathan on a sofa, and saying between the whiffs of a scented cigarette that martyrdom is martyrdom in some respects, has seized on and mastered all more delicate considerations in the mind. It is unwise in a poet to goad the sleeping lion of laughter.

In less dexterous hands the decadent idea, what there was of it, went entirely to pieces, which nobody has troubled to pick up. Oddly enough (unless this be always the Nemesis of excess) it began to be insupportable in the very ways in which it claimed specially to be subtle and tactful; in the feeling for different art-forms, in the welding of subject and style, in the appropriateness of the epithet and the unity of the mood. Wilde himself wrote some things that were not immorality, but merely bad taste; not the bad taste of the conservative suburbs, which merely means anything violent or shocking, but real bad taste; as in a stern subject treated in a florid style; an over-dressed woman at a supper of old friends; or a bad joke that nobody had time to laugh at. This mixture of sensibility and coarseness in the man was very curious; and I for one cannot endure (for example) his sensual way of speaking of dead substances, satin or marble or velvet, as if he were stroking a lot of dogs and cats. But there was a sort of power—or at least weight—in his coarseness. His lapses were those proper to the one good thing he really was, an Irish swashbuckler—a fighter. Some of the Roman Emperors might have had the same luxuriousness and yet the same courage. But the later decadents were far worse, especially the decadent critics, the decadent illustrators—there were even decadent publishers. And they utterly lost the light and reason of their existence: they were masters of the clumsy and the incongruous. I will take only one example. Aubrey Beardsley may be admired as an artist or no; he does not enter into the scope of this book. But it is true that there is a certain brief mood, a certain narrow aspect of life, which he renders to the imagination rightly. It is mostly felt under white, deathly lights in Piccadilly, with the black hollow of heaven behind shiny hats or painted faces: a horrible impression that all mankind are masks. This being the thing Beardsley could express (and the only thing he could express), it is the solemn and awful fact that he was set down to illustrate Malory's *Morte d'Arthur*. There is no need to say more; taste, in the artist's sense, must have been utterly dead. They might as well have employed Burne-Jones to illustrate *Martin Chuzzlewit*. It would not have been more ludicrous than putting this portrayer of evil puppets, with their thin lines like wire and their small faces like perverted children's, to trace against the grand barbaric forests the sin and the sorrow of Lancelot.

To return to the chief of the decadents, I will not speak of the end of the individual story: there was horror and there was expiation. And, as my conscience goes at least, no man should say one word that could weaken the horror—or the pardon. But there is one literary consequence of the thing which must be mentioned, because it bears us on to that much breezier movement which first began to break in upon all this ghastly idleness—I mean the Socialist Movement. I do not mean "*De Profundis*"; I do not think he had got to the real depths when he wrote that book. I mean the one real thing he ever wrote: *The Ballad of Reading Gaol*; in which we hear a cry for common justice and brotherhood very much deeper, more democratic and more true to the real trend of the populace to-day, than anything the Socialists ever uttered even in the boldest pages of Bernard Shaw.

Before we pass on to the two expansive movements in which the Victorian Age really ended, the accident of a distinguished artist is available for estimating this somewhat cool and sad afternoon of the epoch at its purest; not in lounging pessimism or luxurious aberrations, but in earnest skill and a high devotion to letters. This change that had come, like the change from a golden sunset to a grey twilight, can be very adequately measured if we compare the insight and intricacy of Meredith with the insight and intricacy of Mr. Henry James. The characters of both are delicate and indisputable; but we must all have had a feeling that the characters in Meredith are gods, but that the characters in Henry James are ghosts. I do not mean that they are unreal: I believe in ghosts. So does Mr. Henry James; he has written some of his very finest literature about the little habits of these creatures. He is in the deep sense of a dishonoured word, a Spiritualist if ever there was one. But Meredith was a materialist as well. The difference is that a ghost is a disembodied spirit; while a god (to be worth worrying about) must be an embodied spirit. The presence of soul and substance together involves one of the two or three things which most of the Victorians did not understand—the thing called a sacrament. It is because he had a natural affinity for this mystical materialism that Meredith, in spite of his affectations, is a poet: and, in spite of his Victorian Agnosticism (or ignorance) is a pious Pagan and not a mere Pantheist. Mr. Henry James is at the other extreme. His thrill is not so much in symbol or mysterious emblem as in the absence of interventions and protections between mind and mind. It is not mystery: it is rather a sort of terror at knowing too much. He lives in glass houses; he is akin to Maeterlinck in a feeling of the nakedness of souls. None of the Meredithian things, wind or wine or sex or stark nonsense, ever gets between Mr. James and his prey. But the thing is a deficiency as well as a talent: we cannot but admire the figures that walk about in his afternoon drawing-rooms; but we have a certain sense that they are figures that have no faces.

For the rest, he is most widely known, or perhaps only most widely chaffed, because of a literary style that lends itself to parody and is a glorious feast for Mr. Max Beerbohm. It may be called The Hampered, or Obstacle Race Style, in which one continually trips over commas and relative clauses; and where the sense has to be perpetually qualified lest it should mean too much. But such satire, however friendly, is in some sense unfair to him; because it leaves out his sense of general artistic design, which is not only high, but bold. This appears, I think, most strongly in his short stories; in his long novels the reader (or at least one reader) does get rather tired of everybody treating everybody else in a manner which in real life would be an impossible intellectual strain. But in his short studies there is the unanswerable thing called real originality; especially in the very shape and point of the tale. It may sound odd to compare him to Mr. Rudyard Kipling: but he is like Kipling and also like Wells in this practical sense: that no one ever wrote a story at all like the *Mark of the Beast*; no one ever wrote a story at all like *A Kink in Space*: and in the same sense no one ever wrote a story like *The Great Good Place*. It is alone in order and species; and it is masterly. He struck his deepest note in that terrible story, *The Turn of the Screw*; and though there is in the heart of that horror a truth of repentance and religion, it is again notable of the Victorian writers that the only supernatural note they can strike assuredly is the tragic and almost the diabolic. Only Mr. Max Beerbohm has been able to imagine Mr. Henry James writing about Christmas.

Now upon this interregnum, this cold and brilliant waiting-room which was Henry James at its highest and Wilde at its worst, there broke in two positive movements, largely honest though essentially unhistoric and profane, which were destined to crack up the old Victorian solidity past repair. The first was Bernard Shaw and the Socialists: the second was Rudyard Kipling and the Imperialists. I take the Socialists first not because they necessarily came so in order of time, but because they were less the note upon which the epoch actually ended.

William Morris, of whom we have already spoken, may be said to introduce the Socialists, but rather in a social sense than a philosophical. He was their friend, and in a sort of political way, their father; but he was not their founder, for he would not have believed a word of what they ultimately came to say. Nor is this the conventional notion of the old man not keeping pace with the audacity of the young. Morris would have been disgusted not with the wildness, but the tameness of our tidy Fabians. He was not a Socialist, but he was a Revolutionist; he didn't know much more about what he was; but he knew that. In this way, being a full-blooded fellow, he rather repeats the genial sulkiness of Dickens. And if we take this fact about him first, we shall find it a key to the whole movement of this time. For the one dominating truth which overshadows everything else at this point is a political and economic one. The Industrial System, run by a small class of Capitalists on a theory of competitive contract, had been quite honestly established by the early Victorians and was one of the primary beliefs of Victorianism. The Industrial System, so run, had become another name for hell. By Morris's time and ever since, England has been divided into three classes: Knaves, Fools, and Revolutionists.

History is full of forgotten controversies; and those who speak of Socialism now have nearly all forgotten that for some time it was an almost equal fight between Socialism and Anarchism for the leadership of the exodus from Capitalism. It is here that Herbert Spencer comes in logically, though not chronologically; also that much more interesting man, Auberon Herbert. Spencer has no special place as a man of letters; and a vastly exaggerated place as a philosopher. His real importance was that he was very nearly an Anarchist. The indefinable greatness there is about him after all, in spite of the silliest and smuggest limitations, is in a certain consistency and completeness from his own point of view. There is something mediæval, and therefore manful, about writing a book about everything in the world. Now this simplicity expressed itself in politics in carrying the Victorian worship of liberty to the most ridiculous lengths; almost to the length of voluntary taxes and voluntary insurance against murder. He tried, in short, to solve the problem of the State by eliminating the State from it. He was resisted in this by the powerful good sense of Huxley; but his books became sacred books for a rising generation of rather bewildered rebels, who thought we might perhaps get out of the mess if everybody did as he liked.

Thus the Anarchists and Socialists fought a battle over the death-bed of Victorian Industrialism; in which the Socialists (that is, those who stood for increasing instead of diminishing the power of Government) won a complete victory and have almost exterminated their enemy. The Anarchist one meets here and there nowadays is a sad sight; he is disappointed with the future, as well as with the past.

This victory of the Socialists was largely a literary victory; because it was effected and popularised not only by a wit, but by a sincere wit; and one who had the same sort of militant lucidity that Huxley had shown in the last generation and Voltaire in the last century. A young Irish journalist, impatient of the impoverished Protestantism and Liberalism to which he had been bred, came out as the champion of Socialism not as a matter of sentiment, but as a matter of common sense. The primary position of Bernard Shaw towards the Victorian Age may be roughly summarised thus: the typical Victorian said coolly: "Our system may not be a perfect system, but it works." Bernard Shaw replied, even more coolly: "It may be a perfect system, for all I know or care. But it does not work." He and a society called the Fabians, which once exercised considerable influence, followed this shrewd and sound strategic hint to avoid mere emotional attack on the cruelty of Capitalism; and to concentrate on its clumsiness, its ludicrous incapacity to do its own work. This campaign succeeded, in the sense that while (in the educated world) it was the Socialist who looked the fool at the beginning of that campaign, it is the Anti-Socialist who looks the fool at the end of it. But while it won the educated classes it lost the populace for ever. It dried up those springs of blood and tears out of which all revolt must come if it is to be anything but bureaucratic readjustment. We began this book with the fires of the French Revolution still burning, but burning low. Bernard Shaw was honestly in revolt in his own way: but it was Bernard Shaw who trod out the last ember of the Great Revolution. Bernard Shaw proceeded to apply to many other things the same sort of hilarious realism which he thus successfully applied to the industrial problem. He also enjoyed giving people a piece of his mind; but a piece of his mind was a more appetising and less raw-looking object than a piece of Hardy's. There were many modes of revolt growing all around him; Shaw supported them —and supplanted them. Many were pitting the realism of war against the romance of war: they succeeded in making the fight dreary and repulsive, but the book dreary and repulsive too. Shaw, in *Arms and the Man*, did manage to make war funny as well as frightful. Many were questioning the right of revenge or punishment; but they wrote their books in such a way that the reader was ready to release all mankind if he might revenge himself on the author. Shaw, in *Captain Brassbound's Conversion*, really showed at its best the merry mercy of the pagan; that beautiful human nature that can neither rise to penance nor sink to revenge. Many had proved that even the most independent incomes drank blood out of the veins of the oppressed: but they wrote it in such a style that their readers knew more about depression than oppression. In *Widowers' Houses* Shaw very nearly (but not quite) succeeded in making a farce out of statistics. And the ultimate utility of his brilliant interruption can best be expressed in the very title of that play. When ages of essential European ethics have said "widows' houses," it suddenly occurs to him to say "but what about widowers' houses?" There is a sort of insane equity about it which was what Bernard Shaw had the power to give, and gave.

Out of the same social ferment arose a man of equally unquestionable genius, Mr. H. G. Wells. His first importance was that he wrote great adventure stories in the new world the men of science had discovered. He walked on a round slippery world as boldly as Ulysses or Tom Jones had worked on a flat one. Cyrano de Bergerac or Baron Munchausen, or other typical men of science, had treated the moon as a mere flat silver mirror in which Man saw his own image—the Man in the Moon. Wells treated the moon as a globe, like our own; bringing forth monsters as moonish as we are earthy. The exquisitely penetrating political and social satire he afterwards wrote belongs to an age later than the Victorian. But because, even from the beginning, his whole trend was Socialist, it is right to place him here.

While the old Victorian ideas were being disturbed by an increasing torture at home, they were also intoxicated by a new romance from abroad. It did not come from Italy with Rossetti and Browning, or from Persia with Fitzgerald: but it came from countries as remote, countries which were (as the simple phrase of that period ran) "painted red" on the map. It was an attempt to reform England through the newer nations; by the criticism of the forgotten colonies, rather than of the forgotten classes. Both Socialism and Imperialism were utterly alien to the Victorian idea. From the point of view of a Victorian aristocrat like Palmerston, Socialism would be the cheek of gutter snipes; Imperialism would be the intrusion of cads. But cads are not alone concerned.

Broadly, the phase in which the Victorian epoch closed was what can only be called the Imperialist phase. Between that and us stands a very individual artist who must nevertheless be connected with that phase. As I said at the beginning, Macaulay (or, rather, the mind Macaulay shared with most of his powerful middle class) remains as a sort of pavement or flat foundation under all the Victorians. They discussed the dogmas rather than denied them. Now one of the dogmas of Macaulay was the dogma of progress. A fair statement of the truth in it is not really so hard. Investigation of anything naturally takes some little time. It takes some time to sort letters so as to find a letter: it takes some time to test a gas-bracket so as to find the leak; it takes some time to sift evidence so as to find the truth. Now the curse that fell on the later Victorians was this: that they began to value the time more than the truth. One felt so secretarial when sorting letters that one never found the letter; one felt so scientific in explaining gas that one never found the leak; and one felt so judicial, so impartial, in weighing evidence that one had to be bribed to come to any conclusion at all. This was the last note of the Victorians: procrastination was called progress.

Now if we look for the worst fruits of this fallacy we shall find them in historical criticism. There is a curious habit of treating any one who comes before a strong movement as the "forerunner" of that movement. That is, he is treated as a sort of slave running in advance of a great army. Obviously, the analogy really arises from St. John the Baptist, for whom the phrase "forerunner" was rather peculiarly invented. Equally obviously, such a phrase only applies to an alleged or real divine event: otherwise the forerunner would be a founder. Unless Jesus had been the Baptist's God, He would simply have been his disciple.

Nevertheless the fallacy of the "forerunner" has been largely used in literature. Thus men will call a universal satirist like Langland a "morning star of the Reformation," or some such rubbish; whereas the Reformation was not larger, but much smaller than Langland. It was simply the victory of one class of his foes, the greedy merchants, over another class of his foes, the lazy abbots. In real history this constantly occurs; that some small movement happens to favour one of the million things suggested by some great man; whereupon the great man is turned into the running slave of the small movement. Thus certain sectarian movements borrowed the sensationalism without the sacramentalism of Wesley. Thus certain groups of decadents found it easier to imitate De Quincey's opium than his eloquence. Unless we grasp this plain common sense (that you or I are not responsible for what some ridiculous sect a hundred years hence may choose to do with what we say) the peculiar position of Stevenson in later Victorian letters cannot begin to be understood. For he was a very universal man; and talked some sense not only on every subject, but, so far as it is logically possible, in every sense. But the glaring deficiencies of the Victorian compromise had by that time begun to gape so wide that he was forced, by mere freedom of philosophy and fancy, to urge the neglected things. And yet this very urgency certainly brought on an opposite fever, which he would not have liked if he had lived to understand it. He liked Kipling, though with many healthy hesitations; but he would not have liked the triumph of Kipling: which was the success of the politician and the failure of the poet. Yet when we look back up the false perspective of time, Stevenson does seem in a sense to have prepared that imperial and downward path.

I shall not talk here, any more than anywhere else in this book, about the "sedulous ape" business. No man ever wrote as well as Stevenson who cared only about writing. Yet there is a sense, though a misleading one, in which his original inspirations were artistic rather than purely philosophical. To put the point in that curt covenanting way which he himself could sometimes command, he thought it immoral to neglect romance. The whole of his real position was expressed in that phrase of one of his letters "our civilisation is a dingy ungentlemanly business: it drops so much out of a man." On the whole he concluded that what had been dropped out of the man was the boy. He pursued pirates as Defoe would have fled from them; and summed up his simplest emotions in that touching *cri de cœur* "shall we never shed blood?" He did for the penny dreadful what Coleridge had done for the penny ballad. He proved that, because it was really human, it could really rise as near to heaven as human nature could take it. If Thackeray is our youth, Stevenson is our boyhood: and though this is not the most artistic thing in him, it is the most important thing in the history of Victorian art. All the other fine things he did were, for curious reasons, remote from the current of his age. For instance, he had the good as well as the bad of coming from a Scotch Calvinist's house. No man in that age had so healthy an instinct for the actuality of positive evil. In *The Master of Ballantrae* he did prove with a pen of steel, that the Devil is a gentleman—but is none the less the Devil. It is also characteristic of him (and of the revolt from Victorian respectability in general) that his most blood-and-thunder sensational tale is also that which contains his most intimate and bitter truth. *Dr. Jekyll and Mr. Hyde* is a double triumph; it has the outside excitement that belongs to Conan Doyle with the inside excitement that belongs to Henry James. Alas, it is equally characteristic of the Victorian time that while nearly every Englishman has enjoyed the anecdote, hardly one Englishman has seen the joke—I mean the point. You will find twenty allusions to Jekyll and Hyde in a day's newspaper reading. You will also find that all such allusions suppose the two personalities to be equal, neither caring for the other. Or more roughly, they think the book means that man can be cloven into two creatures, good and evil. The whole stab of the story is that man *can't*: because while evil does not care for good, good must care for evil. Or, in other words, man cannot escape from God, because good is the God in man; and insists on omniscience. This point, which is good psychology and also good theology and also good art, has missed its main intention merely because it was also good story-telling.

If the rather vague Victorian public did not appreciate the deep and even tragic ethics with which Stevenson was concerned, still less were they of a sort to appreciate the French finish and fastidiousness of his style; in which he seemed to pick the right word up on the point of his pen, like a man playing spillikins. But that style also had a quality that could be felt; it had a military edge to it, an *acies*; and there was a kind of swordsmanship about it. Thus all the circumstances led, not so much to the narrowing of Stevenson to the romance of the fighting spirit; but the narrowing of his influence to that romance. He had a great many other things to say; but this was what we were willing to hear: a reaction against the gross contempt for soldiering which had really given a certain Chinese deadness to the Victorians. Yet another circumstance thrust him down the same path; and in a manner not wholly fortunate. The fact that he was a sick man immeasurably increases the credit to his manhood in preaching a sane levity and pugnacious optimism. But it also forbade him full familiarity with the actualities of sport, war, or comradeship: and here and there his note is false in these matters, and reminds one (though very remotely) of the mere provincial bully that Henley sometimes sank to be.

For Stevenson had at his elbow a friend, an invalid like himself, a man of courage and stoicism like himself; but a man in whom everything that Stevenson made delicate and rational became unbalanced and blind. The difference is, moreover, that Stevenson was quite right in claiming that he could treat his limitation as an accident; that his medicines "did not colour his life." His life was really coloured out of a shilling paint-box, like his toy-theatre: such high spirits as he had are the key to him: his sufferings are not the key to him. But Henley's sufferings are the key to Henley; much must be excused him, and there is much to be excused. The result was that while there was always a certain dainty equity about Stevenson's judgments, even when he was wrong, Henley seemed to think that on the right side the wronger you were the better. There was much that was feminine in him; and he is most understandable when surprised in those little solitary poems which speak of emotions mellowed, of sunset and a quiet end. Henley hurled himself into the new fashion of praising Colonial adventure at the expense both of the Christian and the republican traditions; but the sentiment did not spread widely until the note was struck outside England in one of the conquered countries; and a writer of Anglo-Indian short stories showed the stamp of the thing called genius; that indefinable, dangerous and often temporary thing.

For it is really impossible to criticise Rudyard Kipling as part of Victorian literature, because he is the end of such literature. He has many other powerful elements; an Indian element, which makes him exquisitely sympathetic with the Indian; a vague Jingo influence which makes him sympathetic with the man that crushes the Indian; a vague journalistic sympathy with the men that misrepresent everything that has happened to the Indian; but of the Victorian virtues, nothing.

All that was right or wrong in Kipling was expressed in the final convulsion that he almost in person managed to achieve. The nearest that any honest man can come to the thing called "impartiality" is to confess that he is partial. I therefore confess that I think this last turn of the Victorian Age was an unfortunate turn; much on the other side can be said, and I hope will be said. But about the facts there can be no question. The Imperialism of Kipling was equally remote from the Victorian caution and the Victorian idealism: and our subject does quite seriously end here. The world was full of the trampling of totally new forces, gold was sighted from far in a sort of cynical romanticism: the guns opened across Africa; and the great queen died.

Of what will now be the future of so separate and almost secretive an adventure of the English, the present writer will not permit himself, even for an instant, to prophesy. The Victorian Age made one or two mistakes, but they were mistakes that were really useful; that is, mistakes that were really mistaken. They thought that commerce outside a country must extend peace: it has certainly often extended war. They thought that commerce inside a country must certainly promote prosperity; it has largely promoted poverty. But for them these were experiments; for us they ought to be lessons. If *we* continue the capitalist use of the populace—if *we* continue the capitalist use of external arms, it will lie heavy on the living. The dishonour will not be on the dead.

BIBLIOGRAPHICAL NOTE

After having surveyed the immense field presented in such a volume as Mr. George Mair's *Modern English Literature* in this series, or, more fully, in the *Cambridge History of Modern Literature*, the later volume of Chambers' *English Literature*, Mr. Gosse's *History of Modern English Literature*, or Henry Morley's *English Literature in the Reign of Victoria*, the wise reader will choose some portion for closer study, and will go straight to the originals before he has any further traffic with critics or commentators, however able.

He will then need the aid of fuller biographies. Some Victorian *Lives* are already classic, or nearly so, among them Sir G. Trevelyan's *Macaulay*, Forster's *Dickens*, Mrs. Gaskell's *Charlotte Brontë*, Froude's *Carlyle*, and Sir E. T. Cook's *Ruskin*. With these may be ranged the great *Dictionary of National Biography*. The "English Men of Letters" Series includes H. D. Traill's *Coleridge*, Ainger's *Lamb*, Trollope's *Thackeray*, Leslie Stephen's *George Eliot*, Herbert Paul's *Matthew Arnold*, Sir A. Lyall's *Tennyson*, G. K. Chesterton's *Robert Browning*, and A. C. Benson's *Fitzgerald*. At least two autobiographies must be named, those of Herbert Spencer and John Stuart Mill, and, as antidote to Newman's *Apologia*, the gay self-revelations of Borrow, and Jefferies' *Story of My Heart*. Other considerable volumes are W. J. Cross's *George Eliot*, Lionel Johnson's *Art of Thomas Hardy*, Mr. W. M. Rossetti's *Dante G. Rossetti*, Colvin's *R. L. Stevenson*, J. W. Mackail's *William Morris*, Holman Hunt's *Pre-Raphaelite Brotherhood*, Sir Leslie Stephen's *The Utilitarians*, Buxton Forman's *Our Living Poets*, Edward Thomas's *Swinburne*, Monypenny's *Disraeli*, Dawson's *Victorian Novelists*, and Stedman's *Victorian Poets*. The "Everyman" *Short Biographical Dictionary of English Literature* is useful for dates.

The latter half of the second volume of Mr. F. A. Mumby's *Letters of Literary Men* is devoted to the Victorian Age. There are fuller collections of the *Letters* of Leigh Hunt, Thackeray, Dickens, the Brownings, Fitzgerald, Charles Kingsley, Matthew Arnold, and more recently the *Letters of George Meredith*, edited by his son.

Among the important critical writers of the period, Matthew Arnold (*Essays in Criticism*, *Study of Celtic Literature*, etc.) stands easily first. Others are John, now Lord, Morley (*Studies in Literature*, etc.), Augustine Birrell (*Obiter Dicta*, *Essays*), W. E. Henley (*Views and Reviews*), J. Addington Symonds (*Essays*), J. Churton Collins, Richard Garnett, Stopford A. Brooke, George E. B. Saintsbury (*History of Criticism*), R. H. Hutton (*Contemporary Thought*), J. M. Robertson (*Modern Humanists*, *Buckle*, etc.), Frederic Harrison (*The Choice of Books*, etc.), Andrew Lang, Walter Bagehot, Edmund Gosse, Prof. Dowden, Sir Walter Raleigh, and Sir A. T. Quiller Couch.

Made in the USA
Lexington, KY
15 August 2013